Standing Out

INNOVATORS, DISRUPTORS, and INFLUENCERS

Curated by Jennifer Bright, Rita Guthrie, and Robert Sayre
Photographs by Terree O'Neill Oakwood

LEHIGH VALLEY EDITION

Internet addresses given in this book were accurate
at the time it went to press.

Printed in the United States of America

Published in Hellertown, PA

Cover and interior design and illustrations by Christina Gaugler

Layout design by Jennifer Giandomenico

Cover photo edited by Serferis

ISBN 978-1-958711-03-3

Library of Congress Control Number 2022912376

Photograph on page 69 by Elaine Zelker

Photograph on page 112 by Tamara Knight Photography, Orlando, FL

2 4 6 8 10 9 7 5 3 1 paperback

Bright
COMMUNICATIONS

BrightCommunications.net

To the incredible local leaders
of the Lehigh Valley, thank you
for inspiring me!
—Jennifer Bright

To my business clients and colleagues who believe
that my ideas and expertise made them better. It's the
other way around. Your energy, your knowledge, your
encouragement, and your connections shaped me.

To our contributors who, by sharing their stories, elevate
our entire community and help other entrepreneurs
envision how they too can rock the world.
—Rita Guthrie

When I am feeling like the world is going to hell,
I take note of the steadfast hard work of small
business owners who produce hope, prosperity,
and a better world. Our contributors
truly Stand Out because of who they
are and what they do each day.
—Rob Sayre

Contents

Introduction

One of the greatest joys of my professional life is introducing smart, wonderful people with other smart, wonderful people. I'm fortunate that the Lehigh Valley is filled with smart, wonderful people. Our Local Luminaries books are all about identifying, supporting, and connecting these people. With this, our second book, we now have more than 60 Local Luminaries! I'm so proud to share their stories here.

—Jennifer Bright

Most of us did not set out to change the world. But here in these pages you'll find that each of our contributors has been Standing Out in their own way. Whether our journey began on a farm or on a college campus, the common thread is that we have each learned how to grow a business while managing from the heart.

What determines our success? Perhaps a simple desire to do better than the previous generation. Most of us have explored multiple paths looking for the golden combination of professional satisfaction while still being able to feed a family.

We cannot and do not go it alone. People and experiences impact us along the way.

I see creativity and community, connections and courage, control and confidence. While chaos and confusion can temporarily derail our forward motion, that is often what propels us into innovation and exploration, and we rise up even stronger than before.

Through this process, I've had the pleasure of learning many new facets of these entrepreneurs and innovators who I thought I knew well, what motivated and drove them to evolve and explore their new visions.

—Rita Guthrie

When we were brainstorming for a title and a focus for our second book in our *Local Luminaries* series, we came up with three words to help us find people who **stood out** in our local community: innovation, disruption, and influence.

A few people come to mind when I think of innovators: Thomas Edison, J.I. Rodale (organic pioneer and founder of Rodale Press), and Archimedes (the ancient Greek most famous for the Archimedes' Screw [a device for raising water that is still used in crop irrigation and sewage treatment plants today] and Archimedes's principle of buoyancy).

When I think of disrupters, I think of Henry Ford, Elon Musk, Rosa Parks, and Cyrus McCormack, the man credited with developing and inventing the mechanical reaper (in 1831).

When I think of influencers, these come to mind: Frederick Douglas, William Shakespeare, Amanda Gorman, and the Beatles.

But what we found is there are amazing people in our local communities who in their own lives, through their work in their communities and for the greater good, **Stand Out.** Their stories were inspiring to us, and we hope they inspire others to find their own way to innovate, disrupt, and influence the world in their own unique way.

—Robert Sayre

I Bring People's Dreams of a Home to Reality

Nelson A. Diaz, President of Mi Casa Properties, in Allentown

My father called me *campeón*, which means champion in Spanish. He always believed in me, and he created the expectation that I would be successful.

When I was just 13 years old, my dad asked me if I was willing to leave Cuba alone to escape communism. At 13, I left by myself for Spain, where I lived in a camp with other Cuban boys under the care of the Catholic church. Surviving—and thriving—alone in an unfamiliar country at age 13 gave me the strength and courage to take many chances in my life.

After living in Spain for a few months, I came to the United States to live with my aunt and uncle until my parents and siblings were able to leave Cuba. I eventually reunited with my family in Florida, and soon we moved to New Jersey. My father worked as a handyman for real estate investors. I was his helper after school and weekends. He taught me the skills to rehab a property myself, which became very useful years later when I bought my first investment property.

Even when I was a young boy, before I left Cuba, my parents expected me to become an engineer. They noticed that I was good in math and science, which are essential in the field of engineering. Another factor might have been that my poor English language skills at that time could have made other fields of study more challenging. Math is a universal language!

I was drawn to civil engineering in particular because I always loved construction. As a child, I spent countless hours constructing small highways and bridges and playing with my little cars and trucks. By studying civil engineering, I had the opportunity to build the real things.

After graduating from Rutgers School of Engineering, my first engineering job was at a small design and construction company in New Brunswick, New Jersey. The owner believed in my abilities as an engineer, and he became

I believe in the power of the mind. It's important to set goals and develop a detailed plan to achieve them.

my mentor. Even though I was only in my twenties, he assigned me very challenging projects that required leading project teams, interfacing with clients, and managing office activities. He believed in my abilities more than I believed in myself! Little by little, he built up my confidence.

Very early in my engineering career, I bought my first property. Out of necessity, I invested in a two-family property, which I renovated myself. I lived in one of the units, and I rented the other one to help pay for the mortgage—with a 17 percent interest rate. Within a year, I sold that property for a profit that was equivalent to an entire year's salary as an engineer. I knew then that real estate investing was the right fit for me.

Over the years, my career in engineering brought me to Allentown to work for PPL as a Project Manager in the Nuclear Department. Although I love engineering, the challenges of real estate really get my adrenaline flowing. I believe that a little bit of controlled risk in life keeps things interesting. In time, the balance had shifted. Today, after working 20 years as an engineer and 40 years since I bought my first investment property, I dedicate myself 100 percent to my real estate business.

One of the many things I love about working in real estate is being part of a team. As an investor in real estate, you need to be surrounded by a great team, from the agent finding the properties, the bank financing them, the title company closing the deal, and the construction team rehabbing the property. Keeping everyone moving in the same direction requires good communication and leadership skills.

As the investor, I'm the "band leader." As a leader, you need to understand your strengths, but it's also important to recognize your weaknesses. Then you can find ways to supplement them with other people or systems.

I have been very lucky that I always loved what I did—both as an engineer and as a real estate investor. I considered my real estate investments a hobby that made me money, so working long hours never felt like work.

The greatest privilege of my work is helping families, mostly Hispanics like me, to purchase their own homes. I work tirelessly to build trust with my clients. They need to have confidence that I understand them and that I'm going to be able to help them. I'm proud to say that I don't advertise. All of my business is generated by word of mouth and referrals.

In my book, the most important qualities of a successful real estate investor are good communication with your clients and your team and fair treatment of them. I'm always sincere with them, and I always operate in good faith.

An especially rewarding part of my work is educating homeowners. Many of the families that purchased a home from me never thought they could do it. I boost their confidence in themselves, much like my parents and my mentors boosted my confidence in myself.

I assisted my homebuying families in getting them into first time home buyers programs, and I connect them with lenders, title companies, and insurers.

I also love to chat with young people who are interested in investing in real estate and tell them my story. In fact, I'm writing a book hoping that other young minorities that came to this country like me are willing to use the opportunities being offered to them by this great country. The title of my book is *Gracias, Fidel*. I chose that controversial title because Fidel Castro and his communist regime is the reason I found myself leaving Cuba alone at 13 and living the experiences that prepare me for who I'm today. I have to make sure that people understand that I'm totally against what Castro did to my country and to the Cuban people. They either lost everything when they left, or they are currently living there subjugated by the regime Castro created and find themselves struggling daily to subsist.

What makes you stand out in your field?

I'm Cuban, and being able to speak Spanish made it easier to create a clientele in the Hispanic community. Some people tell me that I created a niche. Being known as *el Cubano de las casas* (the Cuban landlord) in Allentown is a testament to that.

What are your top tips for success?

I believe in the power of the mind. It's important to set goals and develop a detailed plan to achieve them. When I face challenges or obstacles, I ask myself "What is the worst that can happen?" and "Can I live with the consequences if it does happen?" That takes away some of the nerves and gives me the courage to move forward.

I Love Bringing Out the Best in Other People

Liz P. Summers, president and founder,
Advancing Leadership Consulting Inc.

"To *grow* yourself, you must *know* yourself."

John Maxwell's words resonate deeply with me. In my work as a leadership and organizational development coach, one of my most important messages is: You need to know yourself so you can leverage your strengths.

But do you know where the even greater benefits originate? When an entire organization works together as a *team* to understand themselves, then they can leverage the strengths of the entire *group*. That's where the magic happens.

My company, Advancing Leadership Consulting, helps people, teams, and organizations discover their strengths and work together more effectively. We do this through enhancing self-awareness, leadership skills, and team building. I help people find the best in themselves—to uncover their untapped talents. When people do that, the sky's the limit for their success.

Often clients come to me when they're facing challenges—when their organizations are not firing on all cylinders. It's incredibly rewarding for me to help them think through problems. It can be equally rewarding when clients come to me when things are going well—when they want to level up! I have a high respect for that proactive thinking.

One of my most meaningful engagements was creating and facilitating a multi-year leadership development program with a municipality. They realized in the coming years that they would be losing much of their current leadership to retirement and wanted to plan for succession and strengthen the leadership of their existing talent. It was thrilling to see participants grow into their potential.

Successful leaders understand that organizational development is

I love to inspire people on their own journeys.

essential—not a want or a wish. Investing in your number one resource—your people—is a priority.

COVID put a wrinkle into that.

Suddenly, we were all "safer at home," and in-person communication suffered. Plus, early in the pandemic, many organizations put training and development on the back burner. Yet the irony is people are your greatest asset. That's become painfully obvious with the Great Resignation. People who feel undervalued tend to pivot.

Fortunately, my company quickly found its footing during the pandemic. I can work with people anywhere. While I love working in-person, COVID opened up the possibilities of virtual work. For me, it equalized the opportunities for working with people across town or across the country. After all, my work boils down to one simple thing: Communication.

I was lucky to learn the value of communication early. I thought I was going to major in business at Wake Forest University, but when I took a communications class in my sophomore year, I realized I had found my place. I'd always known that my strengths are working with people, putting them at ease, and communicating. In that class, I found the trees in the Forest. I was home.

I love everything about communications because the center of it is people. As an extrovert, I derive energy from interacting with others. Communication affects everything we do. It's important, and it's powerful. Poor communication results in drama, while effective communication results in success.

A major part of my role in helping organizations is putting people at ease. Most of the time when clients reach out to me, it's because they are suffering from pain points. You can't have courageous conversations until you have comfort—until you have trust. Part of my role is to help them ease their pain. I make people feel more comfortable. When the walls are down and people are more open, they're willing to share, to come together, and to find solutions. When people are willing to let their guard down and become more honest and introspective, great things can happen.

That might sound simple, but because people and organizations are complex, communication challenges are, too. One of the facets of my job I love most is that every project is different—because every *person* is different. Every person, team, or organization comes to me with a unique set of challenges, for which we find a unique set of solutions.

In addition to working with individuals, teams, and organizations, I also teach several communication classes as an adjunct faculty member with the Center for Business and Industry at Northampton Community College: Effective Communications, Conflict Resolution, and Public Speaking. Teaching gives me the opportunity to guide other people to becoming more effective communicators.

Have any mentors guided your path to success?

My parents set excellent examples for me. They are resourceful, and they passed that trait on to me. My parents are also brave, unafraid to take chances in life. Twenty-five years ago, they had a dream—to live in the Bahamas. They found a way to make that work—acquiring a sailboat charter business.

I've had many other fabulous mentors. I worked in advertising sales after college, and Angie Dolan, one of the senior executives, helped me learn the media business, taught me how to communicate effectively with customers, and showed me how to navigate both the internal and external workings of the industry.

After that, another mentor, Denny Kelly, inspired me by her work in public relations as co-owner of an advertising agency. I learned the power of messaging and branding while also appreciating the creative process.

Then for the past 15 years, I've been fortunate to collaborate with three colleagues who are also my mentors: Sarah Arnett, Jeanie Duncan, and Deb Cummins Stellato. The three of them serve as my own private board of directors and co-collaborators. Especially as a small business owner, having this community of supporters is vital for me.

What makes your company stand out?

I easily build rapport and put people at ease. I can quickly read a room and know what a group needs to do to address the problem or take their work to the next level. These skills help me to be very efficient—and effective. I'm able to make people feel comfortable sooner in the process, and that enables us to get to the heart of things more quickly.

What is your work's greatest reward?

I love helping bring out the best in people, and I live for those aha moments when I see someone's eyes light up and they say, "Oh! That's why..." It's a pleasure to help someone discover something new about themselves or to watch the friction between two people dissipate. That's so rewarding. It fills me up to do the best that I can in service to others. I love to inspire people on their own journeys. My tagline is: Illuminating Self-Awareness, Manifesting Transformation.

Caring for Patients, Families, and Our Community Are the Arrows in My Quiver

Michael Carnathan, MD, Board-Certified Family Physician and Founder of Arrow Primary Care, a Direct Family Care Practice, in Bethlehem

I grew up in northern New Jersey, near Newark. I met my wife while getting my undergraduate degree at St. Bonaventure University. She was my tutor. (I got an A.) I attended medical school at a US medical college in Grenada called St. George's University, followed by clinical years in hospitals in New York and New Jersey. I then did my Family Medicine residency at Chestnut Hill Hospital, a University of Pennsylvania community hospital. It was all fantastic training for my career as a family medicine physician.

I chose to specialize in family medicine—rather than a specialty such as neurology or cardiology—because I liked the idea of helping many different kinds of people, of many different ages (cradle to grave!), with many different types of concerns and conditions. For example, one morning I had an eight-year-old in my office, and my next patient was in her eighties. Often, I treat entire families. That gives me an insightful window into their health, history, and lives.

I also was drawn to the thought that as a familfy medicine physician, I could help my family and friends with their health. If I was a neurologist, and a friend called for help with abdominal pain, I wouldn't have been very useful.

I believe that the best way to take care of people is to get to know them. I develop close relationships with my patients. I learn about their home lives, social lives, even work lives. They are people to me—not numbers or statistics. In a world where many physicians are only allocated 10 minutes per patient, I see my patients for up to an hour.

I'm able to treat my patients that way because my practice is a Direct Primary Care practice. We're a membership-based program. Instead of taking traditional medical insurance, people pay a monthly fee for their care. They pay no deductibles, visit fees, nor copays. Instead, my patients have

24/7 access to me—by phone, emails, and text. The number of visits my patients can have each month is unlimited; they can come in as frequently or infrequently as they need. Many of my patients' concerns are resolved with a simple email, text, or call. My patients never feel pressured to come in to see me unless it's medically necessary.

Because we spend so much time together, my patients become my friends and family, and I think they feel the same way about me. Yes, we have a formal doctor-patient relationship, but I get to know them and their families, and they get to know me and mine. Our conversations are very fluid, and then we get down to business and I help them with whatever is troubling them.

For my patients' monthly membership fee, they receive every type of care I can give within the four walls of my practice, including exams, skin biopsies, and in-office testing. I can even do house calls! I tell my patients, "You should have insurance for the big stuff. Your membership with me is for primary and preventative care. We don't use our car insurance to pay for gas or oil changes. Medicine should function similarly."

A huge part of my practice is helping people to get healthier, boost fitness, and lose weight. I love working with patients to help them to identify lifestyle changes that feel right to them. Together we personalize a program that works for them.

My office is very private; we see only one patient at a time, so my patients don't bump elbows with 12 other people in the waiting room. This sets people at ease.

When patients need to have blood work done, get a prescription medication, or have a diagnostic test like an x-ray, I refer them to other experts, with whom I've developed relationships and negotiated reduced rates. For example, my patients pay around $50 for a chest x-ray, compared with the $200 they would pay using their insurance.

I opened Arrow Primary Care in 2019, right after Labor day, after practicing for around seven years in an employed position. Arrow Primary Care has been growing ever since. In fact, it's part of a growing trend of direct care practices. There are around 1,500 of them in the United States, and that number grows each month.

Our rates are completely transparent. The cost for babies through 26 years old is $40 per month, for people 27 to 50 it's $70 per month, and for people 51 and up it's $85 per month. For a family with two adults and two kids, the cost is $200 per month, with $30 for each additional child.

By joining a direct primary care practice, patients aren't sacrificing access to technology. Much like big hospital networks, my practice uses an electronic medical record. I keep detailed records and notes of my patients' health and visits. But my focus and attention is *always* on my patients—not on my laptop. The computer is always off to the side. It's not the third person in the room. It's just you and me, across the table, talking.

In addition to individuals and families, I also work with companies. Right now, six companies work with me to provide better access for their employees to health care and save the employers money. The vast majority of my practice's growth has been employers who want to do something extra for their employees—to support their growth, health, and well being. Sometimes employers can't afford health insurance, but they can afford membership in my practice.

Most of the companies I work with have fewer than 50 employees. I do have a few companies with hundreds of employees. They offer health insurance, too, but they are savvy. Their health insurance brokers realize many employees use health insurance incorrectly—not going to doctors soon enough, going to urgent care, or avoiding family practice physicians because they are so busy. On the other hand, with a direct care practice, the employees have affordable and immediate access to healthcare at a fraction of the cost of insurance charges.

For example, one company with 100 employees has one-third of them enrolled in my practice. All 30 of them also have traditional health insurance. We did a utilization report and found that in eight to nine months, each of those people came to see me at least once. I also answered 900 text messages and 70 emails from them. The owner of the company said, "Wow, they are really engaging with you!" The company saved more than $30,000 in their health insurance costs this year, compared with the same timeframe last year before contracting with my practice.

Their chief financial officer speculates that has been because their employees are no longer using high-cost services like urgent care. Instead they text me when they are feeling unwell. This is proof of concept! The direct family care practice method saves stress, time, *and* money.

How do you put your patients at ease?

I'm very down-to-earth, open, and honest. I don't have a paternalistic demeanor or God complex! I'm also a good listener; I know when to talk, but I also know when to be quiet.

My biggest strength is the amount of time I give my patients. They are never rushed, and we can make sure no stone goes unturned.

What are your plans for the future?

We're so very busy that we're looking to open a second practice in Easton. Down the line, we'd like to open a third.

I also want to become a bigger part of our community, projects, and events. I'm all about taking great care of people, families, and communities.

My Passion for Learning and Educating People Propels Me Forward

Michelle Landis, founder and owner of Pinnacle 7, in Allentown

I have reinvented myself many times in my life, but at the core of everything I do is a passion for learning and educating. I've always been in learning and teaching roles.

As a teenager, I babysat for a neighbor whose son had Down's Syndrome. Working with Danny inspired me to get my special education teaching degree, which I used to teach high school special needs students and placed them in jobs. I had to learn a lot about different business and job requirements, but it was rewarding watching them successfully use the skills they had been taught in the classroom in real job situations! Their smiles when they got their first paychecks were priceless!

Building strong business relationships while placing my students into jobs led to lots of encouragement to get into the business world myself. One day, I walked into Armstrong World Industries for an informational interview—just to see what it was like. They were the biggest employer in Lancaster at the time, and they hired me in the ceiling tile division to sell to lumber dealers in upstate New York. What a rude awakening: It never occurred to me that in the 1980s, a woman selling ceilings would not be welcome into those lumber dealers' places of business. I had doors slammed in my face.

But I was persistent and kicked into my learning mode. I knew if I added value I could win them over, so I learned everything I could about my key accounts' businesses and what they needed to sell more and be more profitable. I took all that learning and laid out a plan for them, and voila, everything turned around, and my territory sales soared! From there, I kept moving—both figuratively in my career and literally opportunities around the country. Every experience was providing new learning and teaching experiences. Anytime an opportunity popped I was eager to say, "Okay! I'd like to try that!" I knew each experience would get be out of my comfort zone and the

learning would be massive. Again, in all the roles, especially as trainer and regional manager, I was teaching, coaching, and helping grow others. And of course, I grew the most, learning so much from each of my team members and clients. And I had a lot of learning and growing yet to do.

The experiences at Armstrong, combined with my newly acquired master's degree, paved the way for me to move to General Electric and manage Jack Welch's Six Sigma reengineering effort in one of GE Capital's largest businesses. That also was a massive learning and education effort, and I was rewarded for having one of the best Six Sigma program results with an appointment to GE Capital's Board of Directors. I then won a coveted CEO role in St. Louis running a small SBA loan business GE recently acquired. Shortly after arriving, we decided to combine three of our middle-market businesses, and I was retained as the COO in a shared leadership role for now, a much larger business.

I began struggling to find my fit and felt unfulfilled in my role. After having to lay off more than 100 team members, I realized corporate America wasn't so attractive anymore. It was time to reach for a dream I had been nurturing for a while: to start my own business! I had already moved seven times, and I wanted to get back to community and the feeling of belonging. So, as Walt Disney said, "If you can dream it, you can do it!"

And I did it!

That was more than 18 years ago, and I am still going strong.

I was fortunate that my years in corporate America had given me a fabulous business education and the confidence to take risks and get out of my comfort zone.

In 2004, after my first full-time consulting project came to an end, I bought a franchise from an Australian-based company called Action Coach. The challenge of growing my own business was daunting but exciting, and operating under a franchise organization added support, consistency, and structure. It helped me build a thriving business, but in the process, I started developing all my own materials, processes, and training approaches and just outgrew the franchise! In 2015, it was time for me to truly branch out on my own, and so I started my new business under the name Pinnacle 7.

The name Pinnacle 7 is a representation of the Seven Summits of the highest mountains on each of the seven continents. The preparations, challenges, and achievements represent the climb that small business owners and entrepreneurs must go through to start and grow their businesses. Running a small business profitably is one of the hardest things I have ever done, and most of my small business clients definitely agree. We experience uncertainty, hit a plateau, change course, take a break, and then continue the climb—paralleling that Seven Summits climb to the pinnacle of success!

I have never felt so fulfilled in my career. I love that I am permanently based in the Lehigh Valley where I can add value by helping my clients succeed and involve myself in the community, too. Most of my business coaching clients are small organizations with focus on sustainable growth. I also began to add a focus on leadership coaching to better meet needs. It was a natural outgrowth of my business coaching because strong leadership is a critical success factor for any business and that became even more evident during COVID. In my business, my experience, trust, and confidentiality are paramount because I need to help each client understand what might be holding them back from their own success.

What's your greatest asset?

I am a good coach and teacher. My experience helps me understand what my clients are going through. I am also skilled at executing through development of measurable, achievable plans

What's your top business tip?

You always have the power to reinvent yourself. Get out of your comfort zone; it will be the best learning you will ever get. One of my other favorite quotes is by Robert Goizueta, a former CEO of Coca-Cola: "You can only stumble if you're moving." I relate to this because I know that my many stumbles have been a big part of my learning journey, so I say, "stumble away!"

What makes you feel good about the work you do?

I love seeing other people achieve, pull things together, move forward, and watch their businesses prosper and succeed. Helping people develop into leaders is a privilege, too. I get a lot of energy from making a difference—and from seeing results. I am the one who ends up learning and growing the most.

What are your future goals?

I would like to move my business to 80 percent leadership coaching on a global basis because virtual coaching is a great way to connect with a global audience and COVID made virtual totally acceptable My mission is to help high-potential leaders accelerate their development and gain extraordinary results. And fortunately, I get to spend a ton of time volunteering now, which I will continue. My newest volunteering focus is as Chair of the Advisory Board of Penn State's LaunchBox Innovation Hub, which offers many different programs and resources in support of entrepreneurship and innovation. I get a lot of energy from helping others and learning from others, so that will remain my focus.

I will never retire. The flexibility of owning my own business and choosing how I spend my time is a wonderful position to be in. It also affords me the luxury to pursue my personal passions for gardening, expanding my wine knowledge, and traveling the world!

Bringing the Magic of Ireland to the Lehigh Valley

Neville Gardner, entrepreneur, owner of Donegal Square and McCarthy's Irish Pub, and partner in Phoenix Hockey USA and Ringer Promotions, in Bethlehem

"If you want to make anything of yourself, you better get an education."

That message was instilled in me at an early age. Growing up in Northern Ireland in the 1950s and 1960s, I was one of the first kids in my family not only to go to university, but to go to grammar school, a university track education. My family taught me that if you want to make an impact, you need the proper schooling.

"Well, no one is going to help me," I thought. "I'd better get on with it."

As a boy in Ireland, I was very into school—well the sports part of school! I played football, and later rugby and hockey, which Americans call field hockey. I was selected to play junior level hockey for the Irish Junior National Team, and then in university I continued to play hockey at club, and inter-provincial levels. I was much more interested in sports than studying.

That turned out not to be a bad thing. Hockey opened up many doors for me. It connected me with like-minded people, and it introduced me to lifelong friends and a lifelong love of the sport. I graduated with a degree in civil engineering from Queens University in Belfast. In 1978, I came to America with a touring hockey team and met a girl—the girl who would later become my wife. Linda played hockey for the Lehigh Valley Ladies, and our common goals and interests grew from there. After a long-distance relationship for a year, we married in Bethlehem in 1979, and we have lived in the area since that time.

After 10 years in engineering, I decided it was time to start my own business. I always had an entrepreneurial spirit, and I was always on the lookout for business ideas. On a trip with my wife's family to Ireland, I saw Irish companies selling products that I thought would sell in the United States, and this started my idea to import Irish products and distribute them throughout the United States.

In 1985, I found a small storefront in Bethlehem behind the Sun Inn courtyard and opened Donegal Square. Although didn't have a retail background, I had helped my mother in Ireland operate a dress shop, and I followed her lead. I just figured it out as I went along, guided by common sense. The first few months were hard, but then the second Musikfest took place in downtown Bethlehem. We sold more in those 10 days than we sold the previous six months! We then moved Donegal Square to Main Street, and in 1996, we took advantage of an opportunity to buy the building where we are currently located, and the possibility for greater business ideas exploded. My parents died and left me with a wee house in Ireland, which I sold to help fund the purchase of our property at 534 Main Street.

Always eager for interesting, new opportunities, I helped start the Celtic Classic Festival. I saw this as a great way to share my heritage with the many Irish in the Lehigh Valley. While many local people with Irish heritage only associated their ancestry with the shamrock, my interest was more directed at helping others to understand the deep cultural and historic ties we have locally to Ireland. I saw the Celtic Classic's mission to introduce people to traditional Irish foods as an expansion of my interests, and it gave me a way to expand Donegal Square with a tea room. My intention with the larger location was to expand and open an Irish tearoom and bakery—Granny McCarthy's Tea Room was born.

I didn't have a restaurant background, but with a healthy dose of common sense and my drive to succeed, and learning from more experienced business owners, I found my way. Over the years, Donegal Square continued to thrive, and our tea room brought more customers eager to enjoy fresh Irish soups, breads, scones, and pastries.

In 2008, like so many businesses, we hit a speedbump. But that pause gave me time to reflect, I decided totransform the tearoom into an Irish Pub: McCarthy's Irish Pub.

That turned out to be a lucky decision, In fact, throughout my life, I've always been lucky, finding myself at the right place at the right time. I credit a lot of my success to the fact that my wife and I have always encouraged each other. I supported our family while she attended law school, and she has always supported my businesses. Many decades ago, I moved to America, leaving my family, friends, job, and sports—all in the name of love. I figured if it didn't work out, I could always move back: Ireland isn't going anywhere! The business also provided me with the ability to travel to Ireland on a regular basis, and through the development of our tour business to Scotland and Ireland, I found another way to share my background and cultural experiences with others.

My life is guided by my willingness to take chances, and making that huge change empowered me to take advantage of many other big opportunities in my life.

"If I could do that, what can't I do?" I often thought. I look at new ideas and opportunities with the spirit of "What's the worst that could happen?" Most of the time, I find the better question is, "What's the best that could happen," because that's often what actually happens.

What have been your greatest strengths?

My foundation has always been my education and my ability to deal with people (a family trait), obviously the retail and restaurant business require a lot of tolerance, patience, and friendliness. I also have a knack for handling money. I have the ability to think and plan long-range. My upbringing gifted me with the value of a strong work ethic. I've never been afraid to get my hands dirty and make something happen. In the retail shop, my interaction with customers, who are choosing a kilt or a handmade sweater, often makes the difference in their experience and in their purchases. Likewise, in the pub, walking through the dining area and touching tables and engaging customers is valuable in their understanding the importance of the Irish culture to their experience in the Pub.

What's your top business tip?

It's critical to attract the right people, to build the right team. I strive to find the employees who share my mission, understand my goals, and work with me to meet them. Engaging employees to see and be a part of your own vision is key to whether you can build your business. Sometimes this means helping employees through a personal crisis, or understanding their strengths and limitations, and a willingness to shift things around to accommodate the personal needs of employees.

What are your future hopes?

My hope is that my businesses continue to grow. Part of the motivation for opening Donegal Square and McCarthy's Irish Pub has been to educate people about Northern Ireland and hopefully help improve the political situation there I also wish that I continue to be healthy so that I can savor the later parts of my life that I worked so hard to enjoy.

An Integral Part of the Economy, Bartering Benefits Lehigh Valley Businesses

Maria Wirth, managing director, Business Owners Trade Alliance

A lifelong entrepreneur, I started my first business just a few years after graduating from college. I had limited startup capital but believed creative thinking could get around that. Solutions like bartering. One day, someone approached me and asked if I'd like to barter with them. Of course I said yes. At first, I bartered to get things I couldn't have afforded otherwise, but even when I was doing well financially, it still made sense to save cash. I was getting what I wanted and benefiting someone else in the process. I never realized that this was just the beginning. My love for bartering would take me to where I am today.

I ran my first business with my husband at the time for 15 years. Historic Impressions, a museum reproduction company, became quite well known at local shows like the Celtic Classic and Musikfest, but we also toured the country and visited Europe for the business.

After separating from my husband, I started another business that experienced tremendous success. Unfortunately, in 2009, the country was faced with a recession that hit my business hard. The economy was in dire financial crisis. Banks stopped loaning money, and my business relied on this.

In exploring new business opportunities, my mind was opened up to a world of possibilities when I learned about barter companies. They have been around for more than 50 years, facilitating barter transactions. Like most people, I had never heard of businesses using trade dollars that are equal to the American dollar to eliminate the obstacles of one on one trade. Organized commercial bartering made so much sense to me, especially at a time when many businesses were hurting for customers and afraid to spend their hard-earned cash.

*When people ask me why you do
what you do, I'm reminded of my love
for entrepreneurs and the struggles I think
bartering can help them solve.*

I believed a barter company would be a perfect fit for the Lehigh Valley with so many great businesses located around us. It would generate additional revenue for local businesses and give everyone involved an edge over their competition.

In 2010, I met the perfect business partner. Scott Martz had been involved in business consulting and sales for several years, working with companies throughout the United States and Canada. He understood the financial and marketing challenges faced by so many business owners.

Together, we were inspired to launch Business Owners Trade Alliance. Twelve years later, we're at an exciting place having helped so many businesses get to the next level using trade. We are proud to offer a solution unlike any other, one that attracts new customers, funds faster growth, and saves operating capital all at the same time.

As a member of the International Reciprocal Trade Association, this equates to trade opportunities for our members with more than 75,000 businesses worldwide. I was honored to be appointed to the board of IRTA in 2020 based on my contributions and passion for the industry.

Our members use barter to leverage unsold time, capacity, and inventory. We help book appointments, drive customers into stores and restaurants, and promote products of all kinds. We work with companies in a variety of sectors, including advertising and marketing, auto and transportation, IT, cleaning, construction, health and wellness, restaurants, entertainment, and travel.

The onboarding process is quite simple. We set up a trade account and business profile for each new member. Similar to online banking, funds are transferred from one account to another when a sale is made. Our barter software features an accounting system that tracks barter sales and purchases. There's an online marketplace where members can search for needed products and services and advertise their business. A member who earns $5,000 in trade sales can turn around and use that earned trade for anything in the marketplace.

The work a company does for other members becomes part of their portfolio. Members become a valuable source for referrals and word of mouth for one another, which leads to cash clients. Barter sales can represent significant additional revenue and have a positive effect on the Lehigh Valley economy as a whole.

We've seen local businesses blossom as a result of barter. As an example, we reached out to someone who had just started a cleaning company. The owner saw the value of trading her services for the things she needed. Since then, she has used trade for advertising, company apparel, car repair, medical and dental care, employee incentives, and much more. She now has 12 employees using trade as a catalyst for growth.

For many businesses, we issue interest-free trade loans. For instance, an auto body shop needed a roof. We were able to offer them a loan to cover the cost of the roof, paid back in auto body work instead of cash.

We continue to grow as a company and serve our members in multiple ways. We source businesses who provide unique products and services and keep in touch with existing members to understand their needs and wants. If a member asks for something we don't have, our goal is to seek it out. With this process in place, we're able to offer immediate customers to new members and serve the needs of existing members at the same time.

When we meet with a business owner, it's sometimes hard for them to imagine what we can accomplish until they see the volume of sales and purchases we generate and who's involved. It's pretty astounding. We work with startups to the largest companies in the area. When people get their first sale or make their first purchase, that's when it really clicks.

A critical aspect is how trade can do more than just improve someone's business. We help people have more for their family and for themselves personally. The "let me help you make your dreams come true" part of what we do is so rewarding.

When people ask me why you do what you do, I'm reminded of my love for entrepreneurs and the struggles I think bartering can help them solve.

From Working on the Farm I Grew to Helping Lead the Redevelopment of Allentown

Julio A. Guridy, director of the contract compliance programs at the Delaware River Joint Toll Bridge Commission, former president of Allentown City Council, and real estate investor

An important part of my career arc has to do with where I came from. I grew up in the countryside of the Dominican Republic, moved to the Lehigh Valley as a teenager knowing no English, and—through education and hard work—earned bachelor's and master's degrees.

Throughout my career, I've worked to help people both inside and outside of the Hispanic community in the Lehigh Valley. And as the first nonwhite person to be elected to Allentown City Council—and later elected president—I've helped open doors for Latinos in politics.

Growing up in the Dominican Republic, my life revolved around hard work. We had no running water or electricity, and I took care of the animals and cleared the land along the cacao and coconut trees. My job was to keep everything clean and working on the farm.

At 15 years old, I came to South Bethlehem with my stepfather, mother, and two sisters without knowing anyone. We moved into my stepfather's brother's apartment with four other people in a two-bedroom apartment. My first impression was that it was very cold, and the streets were empty, not at all what I was used to at home.

My first task was to learn English, so I read, studied, watched TV, and listened to the radio with a dictionary next to me at all times. I attended classes in Spanish, and although I was 15, I was placed in sixth grade because I hadn't had consistent schooling up until then.

I had an aspiration to become an architect, but school and learning English were challenging, and I nearly dropped out of high school in 10th grade. At the time, I was welding bike frames and making $350 a week. I thought I didn't need more education. But my mother, who didn't got to school past third grade, encouraged me to stay in school, and so I did.

In fact, I accelerated my classes. I was given permission to attend 11th grade at night and 12th grade during the day—with wrestling practice and a job at the boys' and girls' club thrown into the mix. I graduated from high school at 19 and attended a bridge program at East Stroudsburg University over the summer. The next fall, I was enrolled at the university, and my roommate introduced me to sociology, which I decided to major in with a minor in criminal justice administration.

Despite all the work I had put in, English was still a struggle in college. My little Spanish-English dictionary was always in my backpack. Again, I considered dropping out—and this time my roommate kept me on the right track by helping me study. After graduation, I went on to earn a master's degree in sociology with a concentration in industrial sociology at Indiana University of Pennsylvania. I was the first person in the history of my family to graduate high school, college, and graduate school.

And yet, I still struggled to find a job in my field, although I never stopped working. I stocked fruit and ran the register of a friend's grocery store. Eventually, I was offered a temporary job for CareerLink and later began working for Lehigh Valley County Children and Youth.

I also became involved in community organizations and volunteered for various non-profit organizations, including the Hispanic Center in Bethlehem and Community Action Committee of Lehigh Valley and the Red Cross. I helped a lot of families and started a variety of programs, including an arts program, a children's program, and an AIDS outreach program to help people with AIDS with housing, health care, and counseling.

I have pride in my community in the Lehigh Valley, but when an Allentown City Council member bashed Hispanics, I had to step forward. She campaigned on the false accusation that Latinos committed the majority of crime in the Lehigh Valley and introduced a resolution to make English the official language of Allentown. People were being fired from their jobs for speaking Spanish. I ran against her, and I won, eventually becoming president of the Allentown City Council.

Although I never became an architect, I did end up being a part of the redevelopment of Allentown, helping lead the way for the PPL Center, Hamilton Kitchen, the Strata apartments, and other developments to flourish. After 20 years, I retired as President of Allentown City Council, but I still have political influence in the Lehigh Valley and throughout the state.

I'm happy to say that Latinos have more opportunities today as employees and entrepreneurs. When I worked for First Valley Bank (which is now Bank of America), I lobbied the bank to serve the Hispanic community, and they took my advice, eventually expanding the program to the entire bank. I taught a Spanish-for-bankers class in which I taught bank tellers how to greet Latino customers and how to say phrases like "checking account" and "savings account" in Spanish.

But my focus wasn't only on the Hispanic community. I worked to help everyone in the Lehigh Valley. I've made great friends here who are from all over the world, including India and Syria. And I've made a point of learning about different cultures, traveling to places such as Europe and India.

Our family businesses have also made an impact:

My wife, who's also from the Dominican Republic, and I have launched three successful businesses. We opened the only Spanish-speaking travel agency in Bethlehem and ran it for 13 years. After selling it, my wife got her cosmetology license and opened two beauty salons. She has sold one of them and still runs the second one.

In all of these businesses, she hired people with the goal of helping them. Some of them were receiving government assistance, and she helped them launch their careers. Through her travel agency, we helped people from the Dominican Republic, Puerto Rico, and other countries who needed to fly home for funerals. If they didn't have money for the ticket, we loaned them the money or provided the ticket free of charge.

My advice to young aspiring entrepreneurs:

Do the right thing and get educated. Education is number one, which is something I instilled in my children, one of whom is in college and the other has graduated from Penn State. Read good books, do good for others, and make God the foundation of your life. It pays off.

What I read:

I read self-help and motivational books. One of my favorite authors is Leo Buscaglia, a sociologist who wrote the first book on love, called *Love*.

Fearlessness and Flexibility Are Keys to My Success

Valerie Bittner, an Entertainer in Bethlehem

Growing up, I wasn't given much encouragement or hope. My mother was often heard telling people, "It's a good thing she's pretty." I set my expectations for my life low. During high school, I was waitressing at a local truck stop.

"If I could just land the day shift and a trailer at a local trailer park, I'll have it all," I remember thinking.

It was a promising sign that I was a terrible waitress. A quintessential example of my waitressing skill was the day I served a man his plate of pierogies, and we both watched in horror as they slid off his plate onto his lap.

A few years later, I was working in the soul-sucking job of phone sales at the Whitehall location of Olan Mills Portrait Studio. In a pinch, they were looking for a photographer at their Bethlehem location. When I told my soon-to-be husband about it, he suggested I apply.

"They'll never hire me for that job," I said.

Then he said the words that changed my life.

"How do you know?" my husband replied. "If you ask, and they say no, you're no worse off than you are right now. But what if you ask, and they say yes?"

And so, I asked. And they said yes! And I've been asking ever since.

That new mindset helped me to change my career path completely a few years later.

I was 29 years old, married with two children. I was having my grey colored at the hair salon when a complete stranger walked over to me.

"Have you ever considering modeling?" she asked.

I laughed.

"Here's my card," she said anyway, handing me her business card from a local modeling agency, which was in Allentown at the time.

With nothing to lose, I went to talk with the agency owner, promising myself I wasn't going to fall for the modeling scam of paying for pictures and

classes that often lead nowhere. In my meeting with the owner, I explained that to her, when she offered to sell me photos and classes.

"If you can prove to me that you can book a job without photos, we'll represent you," she said.

With that gauntlet thrown, I promptly booked my first modeling job with Bridals by Sandra—without the photos and classes the owner insisted I needed.

That was the beginning of an amazing journey filled with opportunities in the modeling and entertainment industry. Most of those opportunities came to me because I asked about them. I'm not afraid to ask, and because of that I've gotten a lot of yeses.

The modeling world is highly competitive. In this business, you're only as good as your last job, so in addition to seeking out a lot of opportunities, I also make the most of each and every one. That's how I stand out in this incredibly competitive world. I make myself invaluable, and I'm always quick to lend a helping hand. If a client needs me to do my own makeup, I say sure. If a photographer needs help carrying supplies, I pick up some bags. Having this work ethic goes a long way in the entertainment business—or in any business. It makes you more valuable.

Another trait that sets me apart is I check my ego at the door. There's nothing worse than a diva. Instead, I work hard at being a team player. I try to be as generous with my experiences, abilities, and talents as people have been with me. I credit my success to the many people who have helped me along the way. And I learn something from just about everyone.

I think that respect for other people is so important because teamwork is critical in the entertainment business. Every time you walk onto a set, you meet a new team. You must gel quickly, even though you might work together only for one day. A diva can make what should have been a quick and enjoyable shoot long and miserable. I never want to be that person. I want to be known for a lot of things, but being a diva is not one of them.

But you do need to have thick skin in this business! Rejection is just part of it. One time a casting director told me I had "fat knuckles." I just breathed and let it go.

Meeting and working with so many different people has been a pleasure. I'm proud that after many years in this field, and living here in the Lehigh Valley, I'm known as a person who knows people. I got that collaborative nature from Rita Guthrie, who helped me radically improve my networking skills. Over the past 11 years, I've really learned the value of networking.

It's also helped me to be flexible. This business has changed dramatically over my years in it. We've gone from schlepping huge piles of videos and photos all over New York City to blasting images by email. I've embraced change and new technology along the way.

Another thing that has helped me succeed is that I'm fearless. My daughter often says, "You're not afraid of anything." That's true. I've worn cobras around my neck, jumped out of airplanes, and spent the night in New York's Port Authority bus terminal—alone.

This fearlessness has scored me a lot of job opportunities, and it's also garnered me many priceless memories. If there's something ridiculous to do, I want to try it! For example, one time for a shoot I rode on the top of a Mercedes through a car wash! Let me tell you: They do NOT use warm water to wash your car.

What do you read that informs your work?

I read biographies and autobiographies because I want to know how people honed their craft. One of the best I've ever read is Stephen King's *On Writing*. He tells you how he gets his ideas and what his process is.

Do you consider yourself to be an educator!

Yes, literally! I was invited to teach a class at Northampton Community College. I was very busy, but I just couldn't turn down that opportunity. It turned out to be harder than I thought because I had to learn education techniques like creating and using rubrics. But in the end, as usual, I'm so glad that I said yes!

What about your work brings you the most joy?

My success has afforded me the opportunity to give back to the community doing charity work. I am the president of the Race for Adam Foundation, an organization that searches for treatments and a cure for Niemann-Pick Type C, I produced the Walk of Hope Fashion Shows at the Lehigh Valley Mall, and I have emceed many events over the years, such as the Leukemia and Lymphoma Society's Man/Woman of the Year, Night at the Races benefitting the Easton Area Neighborhood Center, and the Red Shoe benefitting Third Street Alliance. I was an organizer for the Food Revolution benefitting Second Harvest, I participated in the Lip Sync Battle at the Gail Hoover Charity Birthday Bash, and I even officiated a doggy wedding for the Center for Animal Health and Welfare—that's the short list.

What are your future goals?

I would love to do this for the rest of my life.

I Work to Open People's Minds and Hearts to Transgender Issues

Amanda Hecker, retired educator, cabinetmaker, corporate trainer, and owner of Diversity Training and Education

Many people advocate for and support the LGBT community in the Lehigh Valley, including me. But my real niche is speaking to people not associated with the LGBT community at all.

When I speak to groups of individuals, I'm often the first transgender person they've met or have gotten to know. This is the case even among some people who have friends or family members who identify as gender diverse. I might hear, "My sister-in-law's son is trans, but I don't know him very well." I serve as the person who helps uninformed folks understand what it means to be a transgender person.

People tend to have preconceived notions of individuals who are trans or are part of the LGBT community. They imagine a stereotypical caricature of someone who is trans or gay. But when I stand in front of them, they can see that trans folks are just regular people.

At the same time, I try to influence companies and organizations—whether I'm speaking to people in the medical field, local businesses, school districts or colleges—to integrate the inclusion of gender diverse people into their workplace and daily lives. I talk to them about how to interact with transgender folks and how to approach trans people in their business. For example, many people in the transgender community feel a lack of inclusion in the medical software at doctor's offices and hospitals.

I started my business after retiring from a career as a secondary school teacher. I'm an educator first and foremost. After retiring, I saw that there was a need for transgender education. I wanted to teach cisgender people—people whose gender identity corresponds with their sex at birth—what it means to

I don't consider talking openly about being transgender an act of bravery. I could stay home and hide and act ashamed of something I'm not ashamed of, or I can go out and be an advocate.

be transgender and the impact of bias and prejudice when it is forced into your life because of your gender identity.

This is especially important when it comes to employment. A well-qualified trans person can be passed over for jobs simply because the employer anticipates antagonism from other employees and/or customers if they were to hire a transgender person.

I've talked to transgender people who had successful, longstanding jobs who suddenly faced backlash once they transitioned. There are many cases where gender diverse people have been passed over for promotion or have gotten undeserved disciplinary marks at work after transitioning. Before the law changed in June 2020, it was completely legal to terminate an employee based on their sexual orientation or gender identity. That type of discrimination still exists, albeit more subtle in nature.

This usually happens because of a lack of education. I know I'm not going to change people's minds in a 1 to 1½ hour presentation. But I'm hoping to make them question and think. I've had people say to me, "I'm so glad I know you because, if I didn't, I wouldn't look at trans people the same way." After a visit to the hospital, where I took the opportunity to share transgender literature with the staff, the nurse supervisor admitted that she usually joked about trans people behind their backs but that, after meeting me, she could no longer do it.

My superpower:

As a transgender person, I represent about 1 percent of the population. If I have a superpower, it's to be able to speak to and inform the other 99 percent of the population about what it's like to be trans. When I interact with cisgender people, I try to put myself in their shoes: not just to answer their questions, but rather try to understand where their questions are coming from. That, along with having a skill for teaching, being informed, and being a nice person goes a long way.

How I transitioned:

All my life I've known that I had a feminine side. I thought that I was a cross-dresser and was okay with that. But by the year 2005, a series of events occurred that made me realize that I was not a cross-dresser; I was transgender. I started attending support group meetings for the Renaissance Transgender Association about two years later. However, I was a teacher and a coach, and I knew that I couldn't transition on the job at that time. I wasn't ready to take such a large step anyway. I had been married for about 35 years, and I felt it wasn't fair to my family to jeopardize my livelihood and retirement. However, once I retired in 2014, I felt free to live authentically as Amanda.

Who influenced me:

Many people have influenced me over the years, but one person stands out. When I first met Racquel Hebron, she was president of the Renaissance Transgender Association of the Lehigh Valley. It was my first time going to a meeting, and I arrived as a man with a mustache. However, I had brought along a change of clothes. So I put them on. It must have been quite a sight, and I was very embarrassed. When she introduced me, I apologized for my appearance. But Racquel said, "Amanda, don't worry. You have friends here."

That one statement changed my life.

The fact that I would be accepted, not for my appearance but for who I was on the inside made me feel wonderful. I still get emotional when I think about it. This was the biggest sense of affirmation and allyship I have ever received, and it got the ball rolling for my transition journey.

It's not bravery:

I don't consider talking openly about being transgender an act of bravery. I could stay home and hide and act ashamed of something I'm not ashamed of, or I can go out and be an advocate. For me, a life lived based on other people's values is a life wasted. I'm choosing to live my life.

Other ways I've given back to the community:

I served as vice president of the Renaissance Transgender Association of the Lehigh Valley for many years. Presently, I am on several committees for the YWCA in Bethlehem and am on the board of directors for the Eastern PA Trans Equity Project, which helps individual transgender people work through personal struggles by supplying them with financial aid for food, lodging, legal name changes, college scholarships, and more.

Giving Back, Helping Groups Grow, and Moving Projects Forward Are My Passions

Louis Wyker Holzman, Director of Business Development
for Altitude Marketing, in Emmaus

Growing up, I had so much energy, I knew I was meant for more than an office job. My dad had his own landscaping business, and my mom worked at Day Timers. Hearing about their work and spending time with them, I learned early on that I'm a doer—not a sitter.

I'm also a talker, an extrovert by heart. There's nothing I love more than working with people to solve problems and advance causes. I love moving things forward.

Athletic Training was my major when I attended West Chester University. It's a very hands-on study, which was perfect for me at the time. But during college, I began doing marketing work for a nutrition company. That experience opened my mind up to new and exciting opportunities.

I realized that I loved building teams, meeting people, and learning in a vastly different way that I did in school. Working with the nutrition team, I gained confidence that my outgoing nature could be an asset.

After graduation, rather than looking for a job in my athletic training field, I took a leap of faith and joined a micro, startup website and software development company. It was founded by a couple of graduate students who were only a few years older than me. I was their very first employee. I took a chance on them, and they took a chance on me.

Their business was located in Media, Pennsylvania, but they empowered me to set up my own branch here in the Lehigh Valley. I soon lined up my first client, giving me proof of concept—and more confidence. I networked heavily, doing eight to 10 events a week. My branch grew so quickly that I soon brought on a partner, and together we really blew out the sales for that company. In fact, we helped them to get acquired by a larger firm.

That in turn, helped me get to where I am today with Altitude Marketing

in Emmaus. I was drawn to their entrepreneurial spirit, which was so like my own. I've been here for six years, and I've been a part of their tremendous surge in business. In those years, the company has tripled in size, and I'm proud of my role in that. It's exciting to be a part of this growth, and in turn this is a company that values helping other companies flourish. Altitude Marketing is a business-to-business, integrated marketing agency. We like to say we "start with the view from 30,000 feet." This allows us to holistically look at our client's market and use as much market data as possible, before getting into the tactics at 15,000 feet and below.

That's the right fit for me because I love big thinking. My attitude has always been to say "yes" to exploring new opportunities and to meeting challenges head on. If there's a roadblock, I'll get up earlier, stay later, and go where I need to go to get it done. I try to bring that value to my work and personal life.

I believe in shared-value for any partnerships to flourish I believe we are better and stronger together. That impacts my professional life—and also my personal life.

My parents taught me the value—and joys—of volunteering. I'm busy; we all are, but it's about making time for what's important to you. In my family, giving back to the community was super important.

Today, I still volunteer with my family at the Allentown Youth Soccer Club. All through school I was a soccer player. And today I'm a coach. The Allentown Youth Soccer Club provides mentorship to kids and a high level of soccer—at a fraction of the cost of most programs.

Another opportunity to work with kids and impact their lives is Big Brothers Big Sisters. My "little" and I have gotten together a few times each month for more than four years. He's now a freshman in high school. I enjoy being there for him in any facet of his life.

I try to give back to our community every way that I can. I'm also a founding member and vice president of the Allentown Young Professionals. It's a grass-roots organization providing a network of resources to assist young professionals in developing their talents and in turn foster the continued growth and success of the city of Allentown. I love learning about and being a part of exciting things that are happening in our city. Allentown is evolving, and I want to impact its evolution.

I'm on the marketing committee and vice chair of the Allentown Arts Commission and sit on the Allentown Human Relations Commission.

Another way I serve our community is through my family business, Queen City Realty. In 2018, I bought my first home—a twin. I lived in half and rented the other, which began my real estate journey. Then my mom retired from her career and we began the family business. We bought six buildings now with 26 units, and we're currently looking to scale aggressively. Our focus is on multi-family apartments that support hard-working people in the Lehigh Valley. We love to discover and save older buildings and restore them to their former glory. The mission is greater than just making a lot of money and building a real estate company. We are impacting the lives of people in our community and truly making a difference. Now that is a legacy!

As my career moves forward, I want to continue to innovate and collaborate with community leaders to bring that legacy forward. I'm in incredibly early stages and discussions of planning for some really cool projects. For instance, through my connections in Botswana, we are working through details to better understand how we can take part in the development of the country. My contacts over there are literally building neighborhoods and bringing new technologies to underdeveloped areas. I aim to take a deeper part in this and fulfill my life's purpose to serve a broader community at large.

Allentown will always be home because my family, friends, and business will always be here. But I do intend to move around quite a bit, especially over the next 5 to 10 years, to better grow my network, learn new experiences, and spread the impact across as many different communities as I can. I have lots of details to work out as to how exactly I'll get there, but I do know both here in Allentown and on international soils I will leave my mark.

What made you brave enough to take a chance?

When I had the opportunity to leave my startup job and join Altitude Marketing, I was taking a leap. I was so close to the founders and emotionally invested in the company. While it was uncomfortable to leave something familiar, I focused on the many benefits that opportunity offered, including generous benefits, strong values, and a great work-life balance. President and CEO Andrew Stanten said that he wanted to build a place where even if he wasn't the boss, he'd still want to work there. That's the essence of the company's culture.

What's your top business advice?

Say "yes" to your opportunities and your dreams. The Lehigh Valley is a metropolitan area, but it's not *too* big. If you have an idea and you're willing to put in the work, you can bring it to life. Get out there, get yourself known, and make it happen. Travel. Get outside of the Lehigh Valley, your hometown, and your comfort zone. This will push the boundaries and allow you to think bigger by being open to new experiences, people, and ways of life. This, in my opinion, is the best way to learn and brings such great perspective on life and the immediate community you call home.

I Educate Moms and Help Families Thrive

Patty Gatter, founding CEO of
the Breastfeeding Shop, in Emmaus

When I was growing up in Chicago, the kids in my neighborhood set up lemonade stands on summer days.

"Anyone can sell lemonade," I thought to myself.

So, I created and sold my own handmade artificial nails instead.

Even back then in elementary school, I knew that I would be an entrepreneur. My brain has always buzzed with ideas. I thought so much outside the box, I felt that I should be the one *designing* the box.

In college I majored in communications, and I worked for other companies for many years. But I felt like a square peg trying to squeeze into a round hole. I didn't fit into those other companies—even though I worked very hard and excelled in those positions. I just wasn't content working for other people. I always felt pulled toward starting my own business.

Working outside the home for other people became even more challenging for me when my children were born in 2006 and 2009. Being a mom is my favorite thing in the entire world. And each day that I had to leave my kids to go to the office was excruciating, even though I was fortunate that my mom watched them!

I knew that there are different types of entrepreneurs: Some people buy a company or a franchise, but other people build a business from the ground up—grassroots. That was the path for me because entrepreneurship is in my blood. Both of my parents are entrepreneurs. My mom is a nurse, and my dad worked in biomedical research sales. Perhaps those fields planted seeds in my mind that grew into ideas.

In 2014, I learned that the Affordable Care Act was going to cover breast pumps. A 5000-lumen lightbulb went off in my head! I realized that I could create a company to connect new moms who needed breast pumps with their insurance companies who would pay for them. New moms can be overwhelmed, and I knew it would be beneficial to them to have guidance through this process.

To bring this dream to life, my husband and I took a big risk: We cashed out my 401K, and we had to live on his income for an indeterminate amount of time. The Breastfeeding Shop was born! We opened in a tiny, 300-square-foot place in Emmaus, but our main destination was and will always be online at TheBreastfeedingShop.com. Our first year, I had hoped to sell 50 breast pumps per month to cover our bills. But I distributed more than 250 pumps that first month!

One of my first, and biggest, contracts was with TriCare, a health benefit for our armed services. Because their members live all over the world, our company quickly spread by word of mouth—and social media. Over the years I contracted with other insurance companies, at first here in Pennsylvania, but now nationwide. I was determined, I worked hard, and the Breastfeeding Shop thrived and grew.

Most moms order breast pumps on our website, we work with their insurance company on their coverage, and then the pumps are drop-shipped from our partner warehouses around the country. There is a lot of paperwork and many details to manage. But one of the most rewarding parts of my work is helping and educating our moms. At the Breastfeeding Shop, we don't just sell breast pumps. We support moms on their breastfeeding journey.

Breastfeeding might be one of the most natural, basic things in life. But it is *not* easy. And neither is running a business. Nothing stays the same in business, and I'm constantly encountering challenges. Fortunately, as an entrepreneur I thrive on problem solving and change. Every time my company has grown, I've needed to evolve. We are going through another growth stage right now. It's easy to get overexcited, to run and change too fast. So I try to remind myself to slow down the pace: Crawl. Walk. Run. I recently took a step back and had a hard look at our internal structure. I made the necessary adjustments for us to grow to the next level.

One thing that has remained the same for my company is my commitment to having satisfied customers. I start every customer conversation with, "My job as a business owner is to make you happy. That's why I started this company."

I love those conversations because I enjoy educating people and talking with our customers. When the pandemic started, I realized that many new moms were overwhelmed and had nowhere to ask questions. I started "Ask a

Lactation Consultant" on Facebook Live. It was very popular, and we actually had an episode with 500,000 views!

Recently, I have identified another need. New moms are often isolated at home. It can be difficult for them to get out anytime, not to mention during a global pandemic. I learned that insurance companies are beginning to cover tele-health for breastfeeding, so I started a new division of my company connecting breastfeeding moms with our nurse practitioner for virtual visits. So far we've helped more than 100,000 moms. One mom and baby needed help so urgently that our nurse practitioner told her to take her baby to the emergency department immediately. That call saved the baby's life.

What made you brave enough to take a chance?

I couldn't stand being away from my children. That gave me the courage to launch my own company.

How do you keep your business moving forward?

I always try to keep the following questions top of mind:

- How can my company be unique? My competition is fierce. I must constantly innovate to stay a few steps ahead of them.
- How can we help moms better? My passion is educating moms and making their breastfeeding experience easier.
- How can I tell people about us? At my core, I'm an extrovert. I love people and talking with people, so marketing comes naturally to me.

What is your greatest strength?

I can do a lot in one day. I'm a mom, wife, caregiver for my own mom, and I run a company that sells millions of dollars of breast pumps each year. The amount of stuff I must accomplish in a day can be daunting. But I wake up really early—around 5 am—and start working. I'm a morning person, so that's when my mind is the sharpest.

Plus, because I start early, I can also end early and be present for my kids when they get home from school. That's so gratifying because I started this journey so that I could spend more time with them.

What are your future goals?

My goal for this year is find a strategic partner so I can grow this company and be bigger than my competition.

I Hold the Keys to Ease Your Home Purchase

Jayme Zick, Co-Owner/Operations Manager,
The Settlement Company, in Allentown

Most people who work in the settlement industry fall into it. You don't hear little kids saying, "I want to be an astronaut, a famous YouTuber, or ... a settlement officer!"

It's not a glamorous job by any means, but it is an essential service in the closing of real estate transactions, and so it's rewarding when done right. From the thankful faces of a first-time home buyer, to the investor who expands their portfolio with ease, to the real estate agent who can feel confident that the sale they worked so hard for won't be held up in minutia, our work touches the lives of many people.

But that's not where I started. In college, I was drawn to technology. One of my first jobs was at an imaging company, scanning records and creating microfiche. (I might be dating myself there...)

After a few years working in various fields, a friend of the family worked for a title insurance company and offered me an opportunity. I figured I'd give it a shot. Who knew that would become my life's work?

I worked there for many years, then left the industry completely for a few years, and then boomeranged back to work for another title insurance company in 2012. That's where I met my future business partner, Eileen Aguilera. Eileen is a brilliant, motivated businesswoman who is passionate about the Hispanic community, and she ended up being a perfect fit for our new endeavor.

We worked there together for around five years, really enjoyed the company, the work, and especially the opportunity to help people who are buying homes, which can be both the most terrific and terrible time of one's life! In that time, we observed companies around us growing, while Eileen and I felt stifled. We often wondered, how could we help more people?

So, in 2019, we decided to join forces and start our own company, at a level of quality and dedication we believe our clients deserve. Our personalities

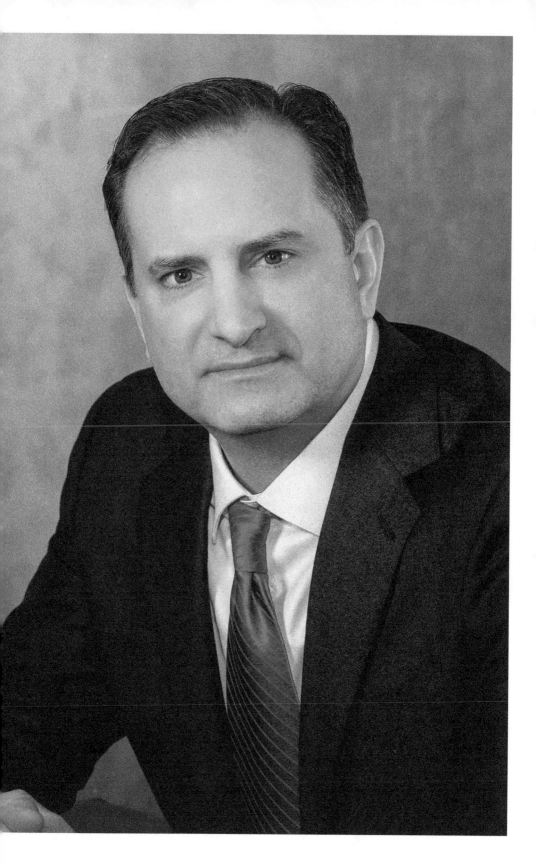

and styles complement each other well: Eileen is the front-facing person who brings in and works directly with our clients, ensuring a welcoming experience. I'm the attention-to-detail guy who makes sure the operation runs as smoothly and as accurately as possible. I like to say, "Eileen brings the customers in; I help keep them here."

Looking back, starting our business at that time was a bold move because soon after the COVID-19 pandemic happened. But like they say, "If you can make it during COVID-19, you can make it anytime." And we did.

We settled into our office on West Washington Street in Allentown. We obtained all of our licenses and approvals, and we went through the final approval steps. We hung out our "The Settlement Company" shingle and opened our doors for business in January 2020.

And then we were forced to shut them again. Fortunately, we can do much of our work remotely, so we pivoted to working from home. It wasn't as fun as meeting with our clients face-to-face, but it was doable—not only that it was profitable!

As owners of a new business during a global pandemic, we worked very hard. We were a lean team of just Eileen, me, and my oldest daughter, Aurora, who started working for us right around the time we obtained our final licenses and approvals. Fortunately, I've always been happy to learn new things and to jump into projects with both feet. I always figured that the more I know, the more valuable I'll be to the organization. One time, I took it upon myself to learn how to do New Jersey transactions. And to teach myself how to do it, I read the rate manual. I discovered that the company had been doing certain things wrong for years before! It's funny what you learn when you read a manual! As Eileen and I started our new company, I leaned heavily on all that knowledge I had learned with decades of experience in the industry.

The network of clients we had nurtured during all our years in the industry enthusiastically supported us as we struck out on our own.

The Settlement Company provides residential and commercial title insurance services in PA and NJ. Our mission is to deliver quality and dedicated service to all of our clients. We research a home's title to make sure it's clear of any liens or claims by other parties.

A big part of what we do is strive to make settlement a positive experience. To stand out among other similar companies, we decided to style our office to look and feel like a welcoming home, which was easy since our office is *in* a house. Instead of trying to convert a formerly residential space to look like a modern business office, we felt that it would be comforting to our clients to make our space homey. It lends a quietly calming atmosphere to a day that can be quite stressful for our clients.

Our lobby has comfortable couches and a TV in the room is always playing relaxing music. Once the final paperwork is signed, a "Congratulations" message pops up on the screen in the room. It's a great moment to celebrate with the new homeowners by snapping some photos together.

But most of our work is done long before home sellers and buyers have settled into our couches. We spend weeks researching the titles to make sure every "I" is dotted and every "T" is crossed. We look for problems that could blow up into big issues at settlement—or at a future sale. While we hope we don't find any problems, when we do at least we're able to address them before settlement. Even in the worst-case scenario, where a problem causes a sale to fall through, I feel good that I prevented mistakes from being made. It is better to know earlier if there's a problem because you might discover this home is not worth the hassle of fixing it.

Most work to insure titles is done behind the scenes, and, if all goes well, most home sellers and buyers don't even realize we've been a part of it. We're working hard to make the settlement feel seamless. Technically we work for the home buyer and lender, but our work affects the seller too—and often the buyer and seller of another home or two as well. It's a domino effect where we're doing one closing, but the seller might be also buying another house, where there's another buyer and seller, too. All of those transactions hinge on each other. It's an elaborate dance and a wrong move can blow out multiple transactions.

Part of our job is education. We work hard to educate our real estate agent clients on the home settlement process. We work hard to empower our clients to be strong advocates for their buyers and/or sellers.

What makes your business stand out?

My business partner is bilingual, and she has a very loyal, large clientele base. That's created a niche for our company. We are very proud to serve the Spanish-speaking community. Also we invest in and support our employees. Employees who are respected and treated well will provide superior service to the company's clients.

What's your top business tip?

Save! Set aside as much money as you can. We learned that lesson when we started our business right at the start of COVID-19. You never know what will happen.

What are your hopes for the future?

I'd like to continue to grow The Settlement Company by maintaining our culture of treating our team members and clients like family.

My Passion Drove Me to Fight for Justice in Washington and Launch My Businesses at Home

Jane Wells-Schooley, cofounder of Dutch Springs Recreation Area and CEO of Northstar Team Development, speaker, educator, internationally certified leadership coach, mentor, and recipient of the National Service Award from the Points of Light organization

In my life and career, I tend to jump into the deep end. No dipping a toe.

In 1978, I was on the National Board of Directors of the National Organization for Women (NOW) when we passed a resolution to have a historic march in Washington DC to honor the work of the National Women's Party in getting equal rights for women. I organized the march in weeks.

I had never organized even a small march before, let along one of historic proportions. It's one of the most remarkable things I've done in my life. We started with the hope of getting 30,000 people to come to Washington, working with women's rights organizations. We ended up with more than 100,000 marchers on one of the hottest days of the year. We had begun the effort to ratify the Equal Rights Amendment in the states. Today, the effort toward federal ratification continues.

Throughout my career, I've never shied away from taking the lead in new roles. I worked as a faculty member at the Pennsylvania State University while being active in NOW. When I left the university, I cofounded an accounting firm and learned marketing and sales. Then I went directly into a nationally elected paid position with NOW in Washington, followed by becoming executive director of the state Democratic Party.

Later, I ran for Congress as a first-time candidate for public office. When I didn't win the election, I went into real estate. I cofounded Dutch Springs Recreational Area, and I'm the CEO of Northstar Team Development.

In my life, I've had to learn to fly the plane mid-air, believing I had enough time to learn how to land before running out of gas. Even when you fail, you've tried something and were willing to take risks to accomplish a goal.

Whatever I fear, I either have to let the fear win or allow the fight for justice to win. When I organized the NOW march, I had the strong belief that people would come and make an impact greater than any one of us. We had physical fear during this time. We received bomb threats regularly. The Ku Klux Klan was outside one of our speeches. Letting the fear win was never an option for me. My passion drives me.

And I also believe that if you have power, your job is to empower others. This has led me to become an internationally certified coach. The most important people to coach at a company are the executives, and coaches don't need to know about the profession of the people they're coaching. We don't give advice. We help executives find their own solutions and their own paths.

I also mentor people to help them with their careers and moving forward in their lives. I became involved in the refugee program and have become the grandmother to more than 30 children of refugee families from many countries, such as Burundi and Congo. My mother told me I couldn't become a grandmother without being a mother, but I proved her wrong. Now some of my grandchildren are in their 20s.

The children and I mentor each other. They taught me patience, tolerance, empathy, and cultural differences. They taught me that love is infinite. It reinforced the idea that the relationships that stand out are the one in which everyone is growing.

My mentor:

One of my mentors was Alice Paul, the head of the National Women's Party and author of the Equal Rights Amendment. She worked to get the 19th Amendment passed, which recognized women's right to vote. After I learned she was still alive, I wanted to meet her personally. I searched for her across New England and found her in a nursing home. Alice guided us in our efforts to push states to ratify the Equal Rights Amendment. I saw her right up until she died. She was a living energy for women's rights. She taught us the importance of speaking powerfully.

How I stand out:

As a leader, standing out is about standing back and standing beside. If the goal of a leader is merely to stand out, I don't think that leader will be successful. I help others learn to stand out. As long as we're learning and growing as leaders and we're offering others that knowledge and understanding, we become a vital part of the fabric of the industry and community around us.

How I've learned to take risks and deal with the consequences:

In my life, I've had to learn to fly the plane mid-air, believing I had enough time to learn how to land before running out of gas. Even when you fail, you've tried something and were willing to take risks to accomplish a goal. I ran for US Congress and lost, and I talked about losing afterward. I didn't feel bad, sad, or defeated. I felt proud of myself and my supporters. I want to convey the message to people that failure to accomplish one goal might give rise to even bigger opportunities. If I had been in Congress, I would not have started my own real estate career, Northstar Team Development, nor Northstar Women Leaders.

The advice I give when I'm mentoring:

Understand time, understand money, and understand your life purpose. You can't have a serious life purpose without action. What do you want to do? When? What will have the most impact? Where can you best serve?

How I organize my time:

I structure my time based on the book *The One Thing* by Gary Keller. I learned how to time block my calendar with a daily focus of doing what's most important first. The most important task is the one that will bring you closer to a goal. During that time block, I don't multitask because the brain can only do one thing at a time well.

To-do lists are deadly for success because not everything on the list is equally important. I'd rather put the tasks into a time block during my day with the most important tasks on my schedule for first thing in the morning.

It's important to remember that there's no such thing as willpower and discipline. The only way to succeed is with planned and executed action.

What I read and listen to:

I have 800 books in my business library. When I have a question, I'll find the book that will answer my question. I also listen to podcasts, including The One Thing and the Rich Dad Radio Show, and NPR. I enjoy multiple perspectives and disciplines. I never want to stop learning, growing, and loving.

Love Is the Foundation of All We Do

George Wacker, owner of Lehigh Valley
with Love Media, in Bethlehem

I grew up in the tiny town of Honesdale, Pennsylvania, with a population of around 5,000. I was always interested in reading and writing—still am.

In high school, I was good at track and field, and I was recruited by Moravian College—now Moravian University. During four years here, I discovered a Love for the Lehigh Valley (pun intended!), and after college I was happy to be hired by a local PR firm.

I worked for that company for a few years, but it was a desk job—not what I wanted to do forever. Around 2008, social media was starting to take off. I created a blog about being twentysomething in the Lehigh Valley. It quickly morphed into discussing local news—often poking fun at it.

My girlfriend at the time, Crystal, who's now my wife, worked with me, and we made fun of everyone, including ourselves. That created some controversy—and an audience. Creating the site was a wild, crazy adventure. It became a satirical site, filled with stories about the Lehigh Valley with a snarkiness no one else seemed to have.

We called our site "Lehigh Valley with Love" as a nod to "From Russia with Love," and to this day it encapsulates what we do. It also expresses how we feel about this community.

For several years, we continued doing full-time staff work and the blog on the side. But in 2015, we took the leap to make our side hustle or life's work. Our business went independent, which was a whole new basket of craziness. We had just gotten engaged, and instead of taking a honeymoon wew started our company. It was a great decision!

Today, Lehigh Valley with Love Media is a boutique, social media company. We help companies with their social media, public relations, and more. For example, we create videos for the city of Bethlehem and Bethlehem School

I'm grateful that our work with all of these companies helps us to help them make an impact on our world. Every time we post a video, we affect people. We take that responsibility seriously, always giving our best to our customers.

District. We're honored to have just won the Downtown Vision Award from the Bethlehem Area Chamber of Commerce.

Crystal and I both work full-time on our business. We're a great team because our strengths complement each other. One of Crystal's greatest strengths is graphic design. To round out our team, we are proud to hire, train, and support interns from local colleges and universities, such as my alma mater Moravian University.

In addition to our in-house collaboration and teamwork, an important part of our work often involves collaboration with other PR firms and local businesses. I didn't start my company with an MBA or business background. I talked with local small business owners and asked, "How did you do it?" People were very generous with their ideas and advice.

As Lehigh Valley with Love Media grew, it was important to define and fill our niche. Many agencies can do what we do, but as a boutique company, we can be more nimble and responsive than most. For example, we recently shot a video with a lot of moving parts that needed to be posted the very next day. A larger company might not be able to pull that off as quickly and fluidly as we can.

Education is also an important part of our work. PR, the internet, and especially social media are constantly evolving, so I'm constantly learning. As I add to my knowledge, I can best advise and educate my clients. We are always looking for new ways to do old things, and we're always seeking entirely new things to do. I've got a sixth sense knowing when to hop on a trend—and when to get out of it.

A part of my business that gives me great joy is our clients' diversity. We can work with anyone. Our customers include a roofing company, financial planner, Airbnb, jazz band, jewelry store, and multiple bars and restaurants—in addition to the aforementioned city and school district of Bethlehem.

In addition to our variety of clients, we also work with clients of different ages and stages of their business. We support microbusinesses all the way up to established long-term businesses. Our sweet spot is small companies whose owners no longer have the time to do their own PR yet they aren't ready to hire a huge agency. We're here to help them learn and grow!

I'm grateful that our work with *all* of these companies helps us to help them make an impact on our world. Every time we post a video, we affect people. We take that responsibility seriously, always giving our best to our customers.

Our commitment to quality helps us to stand out, and we focus on being unique. We love to tell interesting stories, and we're not going to apologize if those stories are controversial. When we see something that needs to be shared, we share it. We're not afraid to take chances. For our company's size, we've had an impressive amount of viral exposure for our clients.

One of our greatest successes is the Tide Pod Shot. Back when Tide thought they had to remind people not to eat Tide Pods, I thought to myself, *If you're going to eat laundry detergent, you have issues. This is something we can work with.* We invented an alcoholic drink for one of our bar clients and it made him a lot of money. He got calls about the drink from as far away as Australia!

My company stands out because we are constantly aware, never complacent, and often impatient. We are passionate about helping our clients. We want to try new things—to push the envelope.

We've been fortunate to have many Lehigh Valley companies take a chance on us. We want to continue to be a positive influence here. It's a tremendous opportunity to own your own company, to chart your own destiny.

Doing My Part for a Better LGBTQ Community, and the Lehigh Valley, Is in My Heart

Lyn Hufton, Realtor, AWHD, ABR, SRS, CRMS, with Berkshire Hathaway HomeServices, Fox and Roach Realtors

I've been a Realtor since 2005. Before that, I managed two Curves for Women locations. One of them was located between a pizza shop and a Subway, which was ironic to say the least.

Back then a lot of real estate agents came to Curves, and one of them kept asking me to be her assistant.

At the same time, my cousin, a broker in North Carolina, said, "You need to do this. You'd be a great Realtor."

I took a leap of faith and gave it a try. After learning, watching, and working with that agent for a year and a half, I thought, "I can definitely do this myself!"

I think being a Realtor appealed to me because I've always loved helping and educating people. As a kid I thought I'd be a social worker. I discovered early on in real estate that the best part of my job is taking good care of people.

I started at Coldwell Banker Heritage, and I worked there for 11 years. Then I switched to my current agency, Berkshire Hathaway HomeServices, Fox and Roach Realtors. It's a tremendous pleasure helping people to find their homes.

More than anything, I love seeing the aha gleam in someone's eye when we walk into the perfect home, and they know it's the one. I love sitting around the table with the families at closing, watching their nervousness settle as the stack of papers to sign goes down. I love handing new homeowners their gift basket with their keys and saying, "Welcome to your new home!" And I love the enduring friendships I make with my home-buying families, watching their children and grandchildren grow. I make people's dreams of owning a home come true.

A blessing of being in real estate is the networks you build. When my husband and I first moved into our development, our kids were little. The development needed a pool manager. I was there every day with my kids anyway, so I applied. Many years later, I've sold houses to three of the lifeguards who I hired back then. I watched them all grow up and get married, and then I helped them buy their first homes. This is a great profession.

A really big key to helping people buy and sell real estate is communication. I've been blessed with the ability to talk with anyone, anywhere, anytime. I have the gift of gab. But I'm careful not to talk my clients to death. (Hopefully!) At the same time, I'm also a good listener. I'm able to listen—beyond the words—to hear what a family really wants and needs in a house. This helps me to find their new homes effectively and efficiently.

I work with all different types of people—all different types of families. A group close to my heart is the LGBTQ community. My youngest son is gay, and my passion for him propelled me into a commitment to diversity.

My three grown children are all very protective of each other—whether they took a traditional route or not. I want my kids to know that they can always count on support here at home. That's the most important thing to me.

I was first exposed to the LGBTQ community 35 years ago when one of the graduate students I worked with at Penn State hesitantly confided in me that she was gay. She was relieved, almost taken aback, when I simply smiled and said, "Okay."

"I was afraid I would lose you as a friend," she confided.

"Never," I replied. "As long as you are happy with who you are, and you find someone to love who loves you back, that's all that matters."

I've always been a supporter of diversity. But after my son came out, I became the protector of my kid. I'm the chairperson of the Diversity and Community Involvement committee on our board, and I serve on the Diversity, Equity, and Inclusion team of my company. I'm also on the board of the Greater Lehigh Valley Chamber's LGBTQ Business Council.

Helping people is where my heart lies.

I credit my parents for teaching me acceptance of everyone. When I was growing up, my dad was in the Army. He served for 27½ years and retired as a Command Sergeant-Major. We moved quite often, and I had to learn to adapt quickly and easily to new surroundings and new people. I learned to appreciate and get along with all different types of people.

Today, I want people in the LGBTQ community to know that I'm an ally.

If they need to have a conversation or if they need someone in their corner, I'm happy to be that person. I work hard to make people feel heard and understood because buying a home in real life doesn't happen like it does on HGTV. In real life, we look at many houses over what could be weeks or months and then hope that our offer is good enough to secure the sale.

What do you read and listen to?

The Color of Law is a great book. I also love murder mysteries (both to read and to watch). I'm enjoying the podcast *SmartLess* at the moment.

How do you put your clients at ease?

I make them feel that I'm at ease. I can do that because I have extreme faith in the people I work with. My mortgage lender, the title company, and the insurance agent all play a big part in the transaction. If I have trust in their abilities, then so will my clients. The people I work with have become good friends, and they have helped propel me in my career. They make me better. This core group has my back, and I have theirs.

The buyers or sellers deal mainly with me. But I'm just the top of a pyramid of people who support the home buying and selling process. I'm supported by the time and talents of the others in the pyramid. We all work together to help the people move into their new home and live happily ever after—at least until they are ready sell it five years later

What are your hopes for the future?

I'd like to continue to hope and help for a better LGBTQ community, Lehigh Valley, and world. I look forward to a time when I don't have to worry about my son and his boyfriend holding hands. I long for a day when you don't have to say, "This is my gay son/daughter"—a time when we need no such designations. I hope that as we go forward, acceptance grows exponentially.

A speaker from the Bradbury-Sullivan LGBT Community Center spoke about how things move and change in the LGBTQ community and how acceptance is very important even if you don't always understand. This cisgender, middle class, white woman is definitely still learning and trying to keep up.

Professionally, I hope to continue helping people buy and sell houses—until I retire and move to the beach!

With Venture X, I Provide the Future of Workspace

Terry Wallace, owner of Venture X, in Bethlehem

When I was a kid, I knew what I wanted to be. My dad worked at the US Embassy in Australia. It was guarded by US Marines, and I was blown away by their presence. I wanted to be a Marine.

I served for several years in the Marines, and then I got my undergraduate degree. After that, I worked for five years as a police officer in the western suburbs of Philadelphia. Some of the finest people I've ever worked with were in that police department. Being a police officer proved to be an extremely challenging and rewarding career. It was evident how intensely difficult this work was on officers and their lives. I can't even fathom how difficult it must be to do that work today. While I enjoyed police work, I wanted something different.

I wasn't exactly sure what I wanted to do, but I knew that furthering my education would help bring it into focus and move me closer to that point. I got my MBA at Rosemont College. It was an accelerated program, but I happily sacrificed my vacation and holiday time for four years to graduate.

In 2000, with my MBA under my belt, I applied to many management consulting firms. I received 36 rejection letters—and one whiff of an opportunity. A fantastic firm called Deloitte said, "Thank you for your time, but we need people with formal training experience." I went back to Rosemont and generated that experience by teaching one of their accelerated classes, negotiations and mediation skills, in center city Philadelphia. A short time later, I updated the team at Deloitte about my formal experience, and they hired me on the spot.

I worked there for several years with many brilliant people, and I learned a great deal. They taught me the importance of being deliberate about all things—including your career. These were driven people who were intensely focused on personal growth and career advancement. The job required constant travel, which caused me to miss much of the first four years of my daughter's life. I didn't want to miss any more so in 2004, I accepted a new opportunity with Pfizer.

I worked for Pfizer for 12 years, advancing all the way up to head of their Global Human Resources Operations. I led a very large team with responsibilities across the globe. It was a fantastic career opportunity. At that time, I wasn't following any predetermined career path. With the speed of change in that organization at the time, there was a lot of grey space. My career didn't fall neatly into any one swim lane. Every job that I had at Pfizer did not exist until I had it.

We had fully developed a highly integrated global function, and the vast majority of the work was done. The only thing that remained was refinement and cost cutting. My interest began to wane. An opportunity came to me to have a critical role in building a rapid growth startup on a global scale, and there was an allure to that. I loved the idea of getting bigger and growing—as opposed to refining and reducing. I interviewed with this emerging company and it became clear that there were extreme challenges within the company, and industry that needed to be overcome. And they were beginning to build a more sophisticated, experienced leadership team.

The company was WeWork. I met with the founder one day in 2015, driving with him around New York City in a snowstorm. At the end of the drive, I thought to myself, *If a fraction of what this person is saying comes true, this will be a juggernaut of a company.*

I agreed to the role and thought to myself, *There will be a movie made about this place someday. I could either sit there and say, "Wow, I was a part of that," or I could say, "How did I miss that?"* I had no idea how their story was going to end, but I knew it was going to be significant. And I wanted to be part of it.

At that time, WeWork had approximately 1,600 people and around $10 billion valuation, but after three years we had grown to around 16,000 people with $50 billion valuation. We were driving unparalled, global growth, which often felt unbridaled and required extreme dedication.

After several years, I decided to leave WeWork. I was ready and excited to recast my career. My new goal became to own my own business, and I was done traveling. I needed a meaningful purpose and to be local.

It took me a few months of research and soul-searching, but it became clear that the right business had been in front of me the whole time. For so many of my career years, I lived in the Lehigh Valley, but I was only home on the weekends. I didn't know much about the Lehigh Valley because I commuted into the city every single day.

I realized there are thousands of people who do that. These hard-working folks get up early each morning and leave the Lehigh Valley to pursue careers and opportunities in New York, New Jersey, and Philadelphia. I know how costly that commute is—in dollars, time, energy, and personal relationships. You miss dinners with your family. You can't coach your kids' teams. You aren't able to volunteer at your school and community. The cost is immeasurable.

But I realized with technology and globalization, it often doesn't matter where you live. I decided to bring the finest of 5th Avenue office space, amenities, and services here to the Lehigh Valley. Venture X, a world-class workspace solution without the arduous commute. At Venture X, people work where they live.

I opened Venture X Lehigh Valley on September 22, 2020, at the Gateway Building at Third and New streets in south Bethlehem. The 13,000-square-foot operation spans two floors, connected by a floating staircase and an industrial loft design featuring stone, steel, wood, and glass. Venture X offers common areas, conference rooms, private suites, event space, and a podcast studio, as well as a long list of amenities.

We had offices reserved before the construction was even finished! But then the COVID-19 pandemic delayed our opening, and we opened with zero members. I spent over a year empty. But today we have 115 members, representing 45 companies, most of which are brand new companies or new to the Lehigh Valley. And we're just getting started.

Venture X is a membership program. Unlike traditional real estate leases, our membership is counted in months—not years or decades. Members have 24/7 unlimited access to the space, amenities, and services. Utilities, extremely fast and secure WiFi, printing, cleaning, and even gourmet coffee, tea, and wine are included, and the front desk is professionally staffed. Our membership is truly all inclusive.

We have a mix of private and facilitated events that range from social to business and everything in between.

This space is about amplifying business success. My objective is for every member to say that their business is more successful because they are a Venture X Lehigh Valley member. This is the biggest value we deliver.

In the future, I'd like to expand to at least three locations in the Lehigh Valley. Members will have full access to all amenities at all locations.

Most of all, I want to foster collaboration between our members. That's what really makes Venture X special. We want to help our members' businesses grow and flourish.

Where Others See Numbers,
I See a Story

Joanne Leasure, founder and owner of
Day One Accounting and Financial Services LLC, in Effort

You might think accounting and bookkeeping are about inputting numbers into a computer program. But in my work with clients, I look for the story behind the numbers.

A company's financials show the flow of money coming into and out of a business. It tells the tale of what has happened in the past and where the company is headed in the future. And it uncovers what a company is doing well, and which areas need improvement.

The story reveals itself through workflow, which is often something that's missing in a company's accounting and bookkeeping. Workflow tracks the information business owners need to get a clear picture of their companies.

I know from experience that it's not unusual for a company's back office to be in disarray. One of my first jobs was to work on the books of a diagnostic imaging company that had been approached by a venture capitalist. Although the company had a good business model, the officers had been writing checks without recording them, and they needed accurate books to provide to the venture capitalist.

Small business owners are understandably focused on getting new clients and managing day-to-day operations. And some entrepreneurs start to beat themselves up when they come across problems with their financials. I feel good when I can step in and say, "You're not the only one who's made this mistake." By cleaning up their books and training them about workflow, I have the power to shift my clients' mindset, help them feel more confident, and give them a clearer picture of their business.

I'm the only local company I know that markets to small businesses with broken accounting and bookkeeping systems. After working with me, my

Small business owners are understandably focused on getting new clients and managing day-to-day operations. And some entrepreneurs start to beat themselves up when they come across problems with their financials. I feel good when I can step in and say, "You're not the only one who's made this mistake."

clients are able to provide accurate financials to CPAs, tax attorneys, tax accountants, government authorities, banks, and stakeholders. I also help with payroll, cash flow, calculating profits, and bookkeeping training.

Having a plan is at the heart of what I teach my clients. I tell the story of when I was 18 and starting college in New York City. I hopped on the subway for the first time and followed the crowd onto the number 2 train to Times Square. When I stepped out onto the street, everyone around me was rushing to one thing or another, but I realized I had no idea where I was and where I was going. It's a lot like the small businesses I help—from restaurants to nonprofits to manufacturers. I help them understand where they are—and where they're going.

How my clients react once I've cleaned up their books:

In the beginning of the process, my clients see me as an angel who came to earth. They're grateful for the help, and they often didn't realize they needed to keep records of certain aspects of their business. However, an important aspect of my job is asking tough questions and holding my clients accountable for the dollar amounts that are coming in and out of their businesses—which can be uncomfortable for some business owners. Some accountants and bookkeepers take the information they get from their clients—no questions asked. I ask questions. "Where did that deposit come from?" "What are your recurring expenses?" I rely on my knowledge and understanding of how business works to pull out the answers to those questions and get my clients on the right track.

How I relate to the business owners I work with:

I started two businesses before Day One Accounting, and I made some of the same mistakes my clients make. Sometimes you don't know what you don't know. As a new business owner, I flew by the seat of my pants, just like some of my clients have done when they started their businesses. I put my business through the same workflow processes I do with my clients.

My superpower:

When people think of an accountant, the stereotype is someone wearing horn-rimmed glasses, face down, clicking away at a calculator. But one of my strengths is my skill at communications. I look at the numbers, and I get to the bottom of how my clients' businesses work.

I make a true connection with my clients, and I take on clients who share my values and are respectful to me and their employees.

My advice for new business owners:

I get calls all the time from people who want to start a new business. I tell them to start with the basics—get a software program and begin doing the work of getting clients and getting your business up and running. Once that happens, we'll talk about putting it all together.

What I read and listen to:

I read a great deal about business strategy. Recently I partnered my brand Day One Accounting and Financial Services with the Grant Cardone Licensee Program to help my clients now increase their revenue, so I am reading everything by Grant Cardone such as *The 10X Rule, Sell or Be Sold, Be Obsessed or Be Average, The Millionaire Booklet, the Closer's Survival Guide,* etc.

Bringing People Together and Fostering Diversity Helps the Lehigh Valley Thrive

Pete Reinke, business development officer and assistant vice president for Univest Bank & Trust Co., Member FDIC, and host of Friends of Pete networking group

People who know me know that making connections has always been my talent. As a business development officer for Univest, my job is to talk to people throughout the Lehigh Valley and suburban Philadelphia to connect them with the right people at Univest.

I have the best job in the world because I'm able to do something I've done for as long as I can remember. I worked for several years at the Lehigh Valley Economic Development Corp. and Ashley Development Corp. helping to recruit businesses to come to the Lehigh Valley. I also serve as a member of the board of the Lehigh Valley Inter Regional Networking & Connecting Consortium (LINC), an organization that helps increase professional opportunities in the region.

My networking group, Friends of Pete, has been going strong for nearly 15 years. The group, which is organized on LinkedIn, hosts a monthly happy hour that rotates between Easton, Allentown, and Bethlehem. There's no cost, no nametags, no speakers. About 125 people arrive at the event every month to network and create relationships that can help them in their careers and businesses. I personally send out hundreds of invitation texts each month.

I know everybody, I connect everybody, and I've been doing it for nearly as long as I can remember. My career and my work have always been about helping the Lehigh Valley business community grow with an eye toward inclusion, equity, and diversity. Having those characteristics in the communities we live in and do business in makes our region stronger and better.

The Lehigh Valley has changed dramatically in the past 20 years.

My networking group, Friends of Pete, has been going strong for nearly 15 years. The group, which is organized on LinkedIn, hosts a monthly happy hour that rotates between Easton, Allentown, and Bethlehem. There's no cost, no nametags, no speakers. About 125 people arrive at the event every month to network and create relationships that can help them in their careers and businesses. I personally send out hundreds of invitation texts each month.

Traditionally, the majority of people who made up the region have lived here for generations. But the area is growing, and new communities are making the Lehigh Valley their home. I see people moving here from New York City, Los Angeles, Chicago, and Washington D.C. and from countries around the world. It's an exciting change that's bringing recognition to the Lehigh Valley.

As the area attracts people from other places, my goal is to make those people feel comfortable and engaged.

There are three groups I try to help the most. One group is college students. As an alum of Lafayette College and a longtime basketball coach there, I've worked one-on-one with college athletes, and I have participated in panels for career services. Typically, college students need some training in how to engage with adults and start their job searches, and I'm there to help.

I also keep an eye out for employment opportunities for people who have lost their jobs. The Lehigh Valley is home to hundreds of companies, and I'm happy to make connections that lead to meaningful employment.

The third group I focus on are people who aren't from the Lehigh Valley. Through LINC, we help local organizations recruit talent from all over the world, and we help those new employees, and their families, settle into the

Lehigh Valley. We help spouses find employment, identify school districts that are a good fit, and do everything we can to help families foster a connection with our community.

You could make an argument that the Lehigh Valley has been late to the party on issues of diversity and inclusion. Other business networking groups tend to segment people—by regional areas or ethnic backgrounds. I work to bring a diverse group of people together who truly represent the Lehigh Valley and help them thrive.

Friends of Pete, for example, welcomes everybody and anybody who is part of our community. I make an effort to include people of different age groups, sexual orientations, ethnic backgrounds, and religions.

Growing up in Philadelphia, I went to a private school with only about 80 kids in my class. My best friends weren't the people who looked the same as me. My friends were from an array of different backgrounds. To this day, I'm still incredibly tight with 14 of my classmates.

I've held on to that philosophy over the years, and it shows in the way I make connections in our business community.

How I personally connect with people:

On a personal level, my approach when I meet someone new is simple: I ask questions until I find something we have in common.

Sometimes people don't want the folks from different aspects of their lives to know each other. People tend to keep college friends, work friends, neighbors, and family in different boxes. I like to bring them all together. And I don't have a problem with criticism. I have faults and wrinkles, and I don't hold it against someone for bringing them up.

My advice on standing out in business:

Show up and make the best of it. Put yourself in situations where you're learning and engaging.

How Friends of Pete got started:

My friends and I formed the group on LinkedIn, and we posted about upcoming get-togethers, local businesses, and charities. I specialize in getting people who don't typically like to network to come out and meet people in their industries and community.

Painting Feeds My Soul and Adds Beauty to the World

Amanda Morris D'Agostino, PhD, founder
of Amanda D'Agostino Art, in Bethlehem, PA

knew I was an artist in grade school. I was always drawing, painting, and building things and then painting them. My dad is a fine artist, so our home was filled with creativity and plentiful options for exploring with my imagination. I remember going as a kid to gallery shows for my dad's work, where I learned valuable networking skills at a tender age.

But when I was a little kid growing up in Pittsburgh, I wanted to be an actor. My dad said that was completely unrealistic, so I said I wanted to be a writer. That went over a little better!

When I graduated from college, I worked in advertising as a media buyer. But that was killing my soul. So, I started my own business as a freelance writer. This was before the gig economy, so as a freelancer back then, I was a trailblazer. I did all kinds of writing for books, magazines, and websites. I loved the work, but not the pay. I was barely making enough to make ends meet. By the time I was in my early thirties, I had to accept that my lifestyle was unsustainable. I'm not a money-driven person, but I recognize I need to earn money to live.

My parents suggested I become a teacher. I checked out the K-12 landscape and thought, "No way!"

I love to write, and at the time I was teaching writing at writer's workshops. I loved that, and so I had the idea to go back to college for my master's and doctorate degrees and teach at the college level. I went to Auburn University in Alabama for my PhD because I found an inspiring mentor to be my dissertation director. While working on my doctorate, I also found a way to feed my creative spirit by venturing into the fine art world via a familiar path to me—photography. As a freelance writer, I had taken my own photos. I already had a good camera, and I love being outdoors, so I started taking nature photos. This was a natural way to combine my love of art with my appreciation for nature. I threw myself into this new passion: reading magazines, doing research, and studying the art of photography. I submitted my work to some contests, and I won some awards.

Then I got into portrait photography at the urging of my friends. I enjoyed it—but only with the stipulation that I had full creative control. I advised my subjects on what clothing to wear and what props to bring. I wanted to always bring my creative vision to life.

Landing a tenure-track professorship at a college is a lofty ambition. These opportunities are few and far between, and the competition for those seats is keen. But anytime I'm faced with a decision, first I do research and identify pros and cons of each choice. Then I methodically review those pros and cons to help me to make a decision. Once I've made my decision, I dive all-in—with confidence.

Upon graduation from Auburn, I received an offer to teach at Kutztown University. My journey had brought me full circle, back home to Pennsylvania. I made a home in Bethlehem, which reminded me of Pittsburgh—lots of hills, a steel industry history, and plenty of great restaurants and cultural activities.

By this time in my life, I realized two things drive me professionally and personally: creativity and curiosity. I make my decisions based upon where I feel more creative and where my curiosity is most engaged. As a professor, I like to bring creativity and curiosity to my students. I need to be engaged, and I want them to be engaged in learning, too.

Another important factor for me is if I'm not feeling challenged, I tend to disengage—whether it's a job, hobby, relationship, or a shrub in my garden.

It's not that my career as a professor isn't a challenge. It is. But over the years, I had the nagging feeling that I had been overlooking the challenge that I was born to face.

Several times, my dad encouraged me to paint. I resisted his advice for years. But my curiosity was piqued.

The next evolution in my journey to becoming a fine artist was beginning to paint. I started to paint mainly landscapes and still lifes with oil pastels. Then after a year, I switched to oil paint and now focus primarily on rural landscapes and outdoor garden scenes with the occasional nocturne (night scene) in the mix.

Suddenly all of the pieces of my personality and life fell into place in a new way. My creative side is fed by the art, and my curiosity is satisfied by finding new scenes to paint. Being an artist is challenging, too, whenever I submit my work to shows. You have to have a healthy ego to do that because it's very competitive.

I've found that I'm able to stand out among the competition, even considering I'm relatively new to this game. First, I'm fearless. I feel that I can do pretty much anything I set my mind to. If I decide to do something, I do the work and put in the time, energy, and effort to be successful. Today, my paintings are selling and being accepted into national juried shows, and opportunities are starting to arrive.

Another thing that sets me apart is my work ethic. I started to teach myself to paint at the end of 2018. In order to produce more competitive and appealing paintings, I'm methodically learning to improve the different elements of my compositions, such as value, line, form, atmosphere, depth, focal point, design, and color harmony. I'm completely self-taught, and I work hard, putting in a lot of "brush miles." Over time, my style has evolved. I'm a representational, slightly Impressionistic painter, with sprinkles of Realism. Driven by my work ethic, I paint—a lot. I recently completed my 500th painting, and that's in just a few years. Compared with other artists, I seem to be fast-tracking the process, achieving greater, quicker success than most. For example, in one solo show I exhibited 15 paintings and seven of them sold—to people I don't know! I was the Best Beginner winner in a National art competition in May 2022.

I've also worked hard to learn the business side of being an artist. I set up my website AmandaDagostinoArt.com and new stores on Facebook at @AmandaDPhotoArt and Instagram at@AmandaDAgostinoArt. I keep track of juried show opportunities and submissions and my sold art. I even track how many paintings I've produced each month as a good reminder to myself that I am making progress.

A third differentiator is my passion. I absolutely love painting with oils. It's not easy, it's very challenging, but I love it.

But the biggest way I stand out is because of my curiosity. It's my super-power. It drives everything I do.

What's your top tip for aspiring creatives?

Don't take rejection personally. You get rejected all of the time. It's part of the game. When I get rejected from a show, I turn around and find more shows to apply for. A rejection doesn't mean your work isn't good. It just means your work wasn't what they were looking for. Acceptance is so subjective. You might get rejected for two shows, be accepted into a third, and win an award in a fourth—for the same piece of art!

Also, find your own validation. I don't rely on external validation. I validate myself.

How have you overcome challenges in your work?

When the pandemic hit, I completely stopped painting. I couldn't create anything for three months. I went into a complete emotional paralysis. I started having hard conversations with myself, thinking, "This is not who I am." I dove deep, found my purpose again, and changed my medium to oil painting, and once again my painting is feeding my soul.

When I create something that didn't exist before out of thin air, from scratch, and that creation touches someone else's heart, it's magic.

I Help Business Owners Bring Their Vision to Life

Byron Roth, Owner of The Alternative Board
and Byron Roth Consulting, in Bethlehem

When most people start a new business, they learn through trial by fire. I love to help business owners minimize that pain as much as possible, by sharing the experience, processes, and tools I developed in my many decades of corporate work.

I grew up far from the Lehigh Valley, in Alberta, Canada. I studied engineering at the University of Alberta. At the time of graduation, engineering jobs were suddenly hard to come by, so I moved to Toronto, Ontario to look for a job. Every day, I went to the library with my map of the city and a phone book. After marking the location of engineering firms, I printed out stacks of resumes and then spent my afternoons knocking on the doors of these firms.

After weeks of pounding the pavement, I landed my first job with Stone & Webster, a large engineering company. They relocated me to just outside Fort Worth, Texas, to work on a nuclear powerplant. A few years later, I moved back to Canada to get my MBA. After I completed my degree, I started working for Foster Wheeler in New Jersey. That's when I found a home in the Lehigh Valley—and a commute to New Jersey every day.

Over the years, my jobs became less engineering and more management. I discovered that my interests and strengths were much more aligned with business than with engineering. I loved what I was doing to help people—and companies—thrive and grow. Engineering seemed monotonous in comparison to the fluid, exciting interactions I had with people in my management positions

My job at Foster Wheeler entailed a lot of travel. I enjoyed flying all over the world to work with different cultures and unique individuals. After 28 years of commuting to New Jersey and countless hours on airplanes, though I grew tired of life as a road warrior. A few years ago, I decided I wanted to focus on the Lehigh Valley and use my corporate experience to help business

owners here. I've found that people in the Lehigh Valley have a rare genuineness. I wanted to dedicate the rest of my career to working with people who are willing to put forth the effort to improve their businesses and lives.

After starting my own consulting business, I learned about The Alternative Board (TAB), a franchise-model company that helps businesses with coaching and peer advisory services. I bought a franchise in December 2019 and launched this new venture in February 2020. Yes, in the beginning of a global pandemic.

I was attracted to TAB because of the market reputation and the systems that it had developed that would be a natural fit with what I was doing to help business owners find innovative ways to do their jobs more efficiently and effectively. My approach is simple: Ask enough questions to understand the critical issues facing the business owner and then adjust my approach to help them where they are. Over my business career, I have learned from mistakes as well as the opportunities that were presented to me. I love helping other people take shortcuts to learn more quickly. For example, I can help them avoid making mistakes with employees, cash flow, or customer deliveries. Most business owners know what they're doing, but in business it's often the things you *don't* know that cause problems or get you into trouble. I can help them with that.

Although I had experience working in a corporation of over $600 million, I have chosen to focus on small- to medium-sized businesses. Some of my clients are sole proprietors, while others have more than 20 employees. I can work with any type of business owner. The key for me is working with a business owner who wants to improve and will put in the work.

Often when business owners come to me, they are facing a challenging problem. In the chaos, confusion abounds and there can be a lot of emotion! I'm able to give my clients perspective, to take a step back and see the bigger picture. I then work with them to have and celebrate some little wins. Those successes build momentum, and suddenly clients understand they have the power to overcome their problem! I like to remind them: How do you eat an elephant? One bite at a time.

One thing that I do differently from many consultants is I have no long-term contracts. We work month to month, and it often evolves into a long-term relationship. I believe that working this way builds trust and the assurance that I am bringing my best every single day to keep earning their business. I want to prove my value each and every month.

One of my favorite parts of my work is assembling and running peer advisory boards. I gather a group of small business owners, and we meet monthly, for four hours. They act as each other's board of directors.

To assemble a peer advisory group, I choose businesses that are at the same stage and level of complexity, such as one group of newer companies and another group of more veteran companies. But the companies within the group are very diverse, and I make sure that we have no competitors in the same group. For example, a peer advisor group might include a human resources company, an engineering firm, a service company, and a manufacturer. These owners of very different businesses each offer unique experiences and perspectives.

Four hours each month might sound like a large time commitment, and sometimes business owners say, "I don't have four hours each month!" Too often business owners are strapped for resources, and they are so focused on working *in* their business, they don't take time to work *on* their business. Besides being a great resource to help solve problems or evaluate opportunities, our peer advisory groups help business owners by taking them away from their business to think about and work on their business. These meetings provide a forum to ask for and offer advice. The owners challenge each other's assumptions and celebrate each other's successes. Strong relationships form, and enduring bonds are built. These peer advisory groups are so beneficial that the average length of stay in a TAB advisory group is 4.5 years.

Just as I help my clients grow and change, my business has grown as well. We all need to change and innovate. Last year, I took a course to become a certified exit planning advisor (CEPA). Prior to COVID, I observed that almost no business owners thought about what would happen to their businesses if they're no longer here. COVID got us all thinking about this, so it's an emerging need.

I believe it is critical for business owners to have a personal vision. Why did you get into the business? What do you want to accomplish? What does your future look like? I encourage my clients to write their vision and display it so they can see it and remind themselves. It's also helpful to give it to a friend who can periodically check in with you and hold you accountable.

Working on your business is a journey that takes time and focus. Be purposeful and diligent. Identify a few key goals and then break them into manageable tasks.

Looking ahead, my goal is to double or even triple the work I'm doing, but at the same time I want to preserve the personal one-on-one relationships I build with my clients. I look forward to helping even more business owners figure out what their own futures hold.

When Emotions Run High at Closings, I'm a Positive Voice in the Settlement Room

Carmen S. Dancsecs, business development manager,
First United Land Transfer, in Allentown

I n the world of title insurance, an important part of the job is controlling the room.

Buying or selling a home is typically a stressful situation, and I see all of the emotions—from excitement about being first-time buyers to nervousness over the buying process to sadness at selling a childhood home. Part of my job is to keep people calm and reassured that everything will be okay, even if unexpected situations arise.

There's an abundance of information that's foreign to many buyers and sellers at a settlement, and I'm responsible for explaining the process. People are nervous, and I can either keep them calm or make them more nervous.

Things don't always work out the way we hoped. At one closing that had already been prolonged, the seller arrived without identification. We couldn't go forward without her valid ID, and I had to tell the buyers the closing couldn't happen—at that moment, but I assured them that things would work out in the end. I'm a positive voice, and that allows my career to flourish.

However, meeting the buyers and sellers is the last step in the process of my job. A large part of my responsibility is creating and maintaining relationships with lenders and realtors. Our processing department handles the title search, tax liens, checks that water and sewer are up to date, escrows are current, and makes sure that everything that needs to be paid off or that is the buyer's responsibility is taken care of. By the time we get to settlement, issues have been resolved, and the settlement is a smooth process.

I understand the process of buying a home is hard work for many people and not something to take for granted. I'm a single mom, and when I got divorced, I lost my home. But in 2020, I was able to build a home for myself and my children. I encourage everyone, whether they're divorced or a single mom or single dad, that they can do it.

Our bilingual services make us stand out in the Lehigh Valley:

One way First United Land Transfer and my services stand out in the Lehigh Valley is because we serve the Latino community and other communities who are migrating to the Lehigh Valley, which is typically an underserved population.

I've done closings in both English and Spanish, our processors speak Spanish, and we have internal documents translated to Spanish for our clients. Some Realtors come to us specifically because we can communicate effectively with their Spanish-speaking clients.

My passion is with people:

I come from a family of nurses, doctors, pastors, and some engineers. When I was younger, I thought I'd end up in the medical field. But as I got older, I realized my passion was with people and that I wanted to help people in a different way. I spent 12 years in the beauty industry before making the move to title insurance. After working with another title agency, I joined First United Land Transfer in 2021. Since then, I've assisted in hundreds of settlements to date—about 30 to 40 settlements a week.

As I transitioned to title insurance, I knew it was the right industry for me because I excel at customer service. Working with people directly and helping them—watching them get the key to their new home—is the best part of my job. Our clients share their stories with us. Some never thought they'd own a home. Families come dressed up, with their kids wearing matching dresses, for the momentous occasion. I see the buyer's hand shaking as they sign the paperwork. Some burst into tears at the end of the process. It's a privilege that I'm able to impact so many people.

I'm an encouraging voice because I relate to my clients:

Another way I stand out in title insurance is because of the way I conduct my job. Our Realtors and lenders know they can call me at any time, whether it's 1 p.m. or 1 a.m. If they're up, I'm up. I literally work around the clock.

I understand the process of buying a home is hard work for many people and not something to take for granted. I'm a single mom, and when I got divorced, I lost my home. But in 2020, I was able to build a home for myself and my children. I encourage everyone, whether they're divorced or a single mom or single dad, that they can do it.

I'm supported in industry, and I work to support others:

First United Land Transfer is a perfect fit for me because the company treats everyone like family. We bring warm chocolate chip cookies to every closing. Everything we do, we do with excellence. Nobody becomes successful on their own, and I have a great support system within my company to push me and keep me on track.

At the same time, I work to help others excel as well. I'm a mentor to some of the younger people in my office. I'm teaching them how to do closings, work with people, and create events.

My daily schedule:

I have a daily schedule that I prepare for, but the truth is that I have to be ready for anything. Closings may be canceled or added at the last minute. You can't be a creature of habit in my job.

What I read:

I deal with so many people on a regular basis that I like to read books on business development and relationships. A recent book I've read is the *Seven Levels of Communication* by Michael Maher. I also keep up to date on the intricacies of title insurance.

I Strengthen My Organization Through My Own Continued Learning

David C. Myers, Senior Human Resources/Labor
Relations Leader, in Kutztown

A lot of what I needed to know about business I learned as a golf caddy starting at age 11. Not really, but that *is* where a lot of my early business education was developed.

I worked as a caddy all through junior high, high school, and college. It was very rewarding and enjoyable. Most of the people I caddied for were senior executives in local businesses in my hometown of Latrobe, Pennsylvania. If I walked in front of them, I could listen to their conversations. I soaked up those conversations like a sponge but never breached their confidence to anyone.

In reality, my foundation started with my parents who taught me to have a strong work ethic. From an early age, I worked in many different jobs. Aside from caddying, I delivered newspapers, worked city maintenance, painted houses, worked in a steel mill, and did maintenance for an apartment complex. My entire family was a great support system for me, too. We had a lot to learn from each other, especially for me being the oldest of six children. I married the woman of my dreams, and we had three children together, each of them starting their own families with my children-in-law. And now we are blessed with eight grandchildren. Each day is a learning experience.

With that informal business education as a base, I majored in Business Administration at Robert Morris University in Pittsburgh. Then I achieved my Master's in Industrial Relations from West Virginia University, an MBA from Penn State University, and a certificate in Corporate Entrepreneurship from Lehigh University—a prime example of being a lifelong, continual learner.

My career took a winding road to get where I am today, which provided me a great depth of experience. I worked in public administration for a

I strive to make people understand that they are all important to our company's success. The success I have attained was a result of always being able and wanting to learn, and helping other people improve.

fewyears and then in sales and sales management. Then in 1986, I began my career in Human Resources and Labor Relations.

I think I was attracted to the human resources field because I like to see people and organizations develop, prosper, and grow. For example, one company I worked with grew more than 500 percent in just over 10 years. I worked as an independent consultant for a few years primarily helping organizations and individuals develop, but I missed growing the organization from within. So, on two occasions I went to work for my clients. I've worked for many varied companies over the years, including Martha White Foods, Union Carbide, Americold Logistics, Quaker Oats, Total Logistics Control, Diageo (the maker of Smirnoff), Cigars International, and now Jetson Specialty Marketing (JSM), a direct mail company.

It's ironic that even though I *do* like people and my field is all *about* people, I didn't used to value having a network. Sure I've had friends. But a work network, not so much! My belief back then was to "keep your nose to the grindstone." All that grinding didn't leave a lot of time left over for relationship building, which I discovered to be a key to success especially when you are in transition, between roles/opportunities. For example, in 1998 my job at Union Carbide was unexpectedly eliminated. Suddenly, I had to pivot—and that word wasn't even in my vocabulary. I realized that in those situations, your network is the key to finding new, better opportunities—quickly. Fortunately, I was able to land a great opportunity. But I was not going to risk that happening again. So after that experience, I vowed to create my "extensive network." Today I have more than 1,000 valued connections on LinkedIn.

Another trait of mine that has contributed to my success is that I'm always looking for ways to grow. I hold dear the philosophy of continuous improvement. I ask myself all the time, "What can I do to make today better than yesterday?" I try to be a continual learner. I'm always looking for new and better ways to do things, including better ways to be me.

With the mindset of continuous improvement, coupled with the fact that I've been in the world of work for a lot of years, I've learned a great deal. (Though I don't necessarily consider myself old; I consider myself seasoned.) The certification in Corporate Entrepreneurship is an example of continual learning. It supported me in my personal entrepreneurial efforts and helped me bring that approach into my organizations. In today's world, we all must possess a creative, entrepreneurial spirit.

Now I am the Vice President, Human Resources at JSM. It's a family-owned, full-service, direct marketing communications company. JSM has a suite of solutions to assist in growing any business. This customer-focused approach motivates me every day to strengthen our organization and also to serve our external clients.

My biggest challenge right now is this labor market. It has changed considerably in the past few years, and human resources practitioners are looking for creative, innovative solutions. My father worked for the same company for 30 years. Today, people change jobs much more frequently, and the labor market is extremely tight. It is critical for businesses to stand out to compete for the top talent. Our HR team and organization work hard to stand out in being an "Employer of Choice." Not every workplace is ideal for everyone, so each organization must have their own unique employer brand. Each day, we try to improve our brand.

What's your top business tip?

You can learn from anyone, anywhere, at any time. I've worked with some great bosses who were true leaders. I've learned a lot from them, as well as my family members. But I learned just as much, if not more, from the "bad" bosses or coworkers, from their mistakes, lack of leadership, or incompetency.

How do you stand out in your field?

I strive to make people understand that they are all important to our company's success. The success I have attained was a result of always being able and wanting to learn and helping other people improve.

What are your future goals?

I want to continue to add value to organizations. Even after I retire from corporate life, I still want to be engaged. For example, I participate in 1 Million Cups, and I was Executive Chair of Lehigh Valley Professionals for some time. Lastly, I want to spend more time with my family, play more and better golf, and start fishing again.

I Help People Gain Financial Empowerment Through SMART Goals and By Finding Meaning Behind Financial Decisions

Julie Knight, Certified Financial Planner®, AIF®, CLTC®, CDFA®, Financial Adviser, and First Vice President of Wealth Management at Janney Montgomery Scott LLC

Financial decisions can be complex and full of emotion, and tackling complicated financial scenarios with clients is my passion!

Financial empowerment has many facets, depending upon where you are on your financial journey. When planning for retiring in your 60s, you need to have the peace of mind that you have enough funds to last for another 30 years or more. When a parent or a spouse dies, who's going to handle the money? Has the family determined how to efficiently transfer the wealth of the parents to the next generation without paying too much in taxes? Others may be thinking about the possibility of needing long-term care in the future.

Can you identify your financial goals, or fears? When can I retire? Can I make ends meet and still save? Can I afford college tuition? Is long-term care affordable? Can I leave a legacy for my children? Whether you are just starting out or planning for retirement, I can help you build your financial future with strategic planning and periodic review of your progress.

My experience and education allow me to guide my clients to make the best choices. In addition to being a Certified Financial Planner® Professional, I am certified in long-term care and have advanced knowledge in multi-generational wealth transfer, among other experience.

But there's more to my approach to financial planning. When parsing these decisions with clients, I always work to find the *meaning* behind financial choices.

We all must find a balance between our needs, wants, and wishes. Needs are those expenses we can't avoid, such as housing, health care, food, and clothing. Wants are those extras that make life enjoyable, including eating out, vacations, and helping with our children's education expenses. Wishes are the cherry on top: a celebratory event for a birthday or a one-time, big-ticket item.

To ensure my clients can adequately meet their needs, wants, and wishes, I work with them to set measurable, time-bound goals. Goals allow us to work to live, not to live to work. A SMART goal is specific, measurable, attainable, realistic, and time bound. Ideally, it should include numbers, whether it's a percentage of income that goes into a retirement account or a date and a dollar amount for contributions. At the end of the month or year, it should be easy to look back to determine if the goal was accomplished.

I like to start with milestones, which are the most impactful and usually big-ticket items. They might be a goal to earn a degree, buy a new home, or get a new job. Achieving smaller, mini goals can help get to the milestone goal.

Natural timelines are also a great place to start. We all have Tax Day, so we can put that on our calendar and set goals around it. Goals around birthdays, holidays, and vacations can come next because if we don't put one of them on the calendar and create a "save the date," we might not be prepared, or we may miss the opportunity to celebrate and enjoy.

Goals have been an important part of my career and personal life, as well. When I was 21 years old, I wrote 100 life goals. I take on one goal—one change—at a time. I also create lists that help me prioritize my time to meet my goals. I create a list of goals every year, and over time they evolve based on what I've already accomplished.

Clients have told me that the process I guide them through allows them to feel financially empowered. My clients have many choices when investing money and when to retire. Steering them to a place where they feel empowered by their decisions tells me I'm achieving the ultimate goal of helping my clients.

What makes me stand out in my field:

I've developed a gold standard on the financial planning process and how to implement this decision-making process with clients. I'm often asked by colleagues and management for input on how to educate my peers and clients. I hold educational workshops where I share my experience on topics such as multigenerational wealth transfer, long-term care planning, and Social Security.

Because financial planning is still traditionally male-dominated, there's a huge opportunity and demand for women who have the financial planning focus I have.

How living in six countries has impacted my career:

I grew up on a farm in Williams Township, and I lived in six countries after earning my bachelor's degree. After working in Germany, I moved to Melbourne, Australia, to attend one of the top-ranked global business schools and earned my MBA. I've also spent time as a student in France, Spain, and India.

Traveling to more than 35 countries has helped me with creative problem solving. When you understand that a way of doing something may be normal in one place but completely different somewhere else, it opens your mind to creativity. It's not about seeing the box or thinking outside the box, it's about *creating* your box. Having a global perspective has helped me do that.

I've also felt and seen the difference between real poverty and wealth. Exploring the globe has changed my perspective on what's really important in life, what I value, how I treat people, and how to respect the environment and community.

How financial planning became the right career for me:

I changed my major several times in college. I've always been people-oriented and wanted to help people. I'm also competitive, self-motivated, and very independent. I knew I wanted a job where I'd be compensated based on my efforts and results.

Combining those attributes with my lifelong skills of being good with money and numbers, financial planning has become a satisfying career for me. Every client presents a different creative scenario to manage for improved, targets outcomes.

What I read and listen to that inform my work:

I'm very selective about what I allow to influence my decision-making. I allocate time to attend workshops for financial professionals, such as changes to the market, tax or estate laws, and investment landscaping.

Local connections are important to me:

I'm a board member of the Estate Planning Council of the Lehigh Valley and a member of Lehigh Valley Aging in Place. Since 2007, I've been active with the Greater Lehigh Valley Chamber of Commerce. I helped spearhead the Young Professional Council. I've also held positions such as the Chair of the Ambassadors Council and a member of the Board of Governors. I volunteer for the Perfect Fit of Allentown's Annual Luncheon, which helped the 10,000th woman transition back into the workforce last year.

In 2019, I was honored as one of the 2019 Women of Influence from Lehigh Valley Business.

As a Civil Engineer, I am a Nurturer of Nature, Protector of Property Rights and Educator of People

Laura M. Eberly, PE, LEED AP, Director of Civil Engineering,
Lehigh Valley, Reuther+Bowen, in Bethlehem

I didn't grow up in the Lehigh Valley. I was raised in New Jersey, in an area that is an extended suburb of New York City. I came to the Lehigh Valley to attend Lehigh University, and I never went home. In fact, the Lehigh Valley *is* now my home.

One of the first things that surprised me about the Lehigh Valley was the friendliness of its people. I remember people smiling and saying hi to me at the grocery store. *I don't even know you! Why are you talking to me?* I remember thinking. Where I grew up, people didn't wave and smile. As an introvert by nature, it was new and unfamiliar to me, but a difference I could grow to love.

Growing up, I loved science and math. I thought I wanted to be an archaeologist, but I was realistic enough to know that there's not a whole lot of opportunities to dig up dinosaur bones.

Luckily, my high school guidance counselor saw past my gender and suggested I pursue engineering. Building bridges or coding computers didn't appeal to me, but I love to be outside, and I took some classes at Lehigh on water resources and stream health. I discovered that was my passion, so I focused on storm water management.

Back when I began my career in the 1990s, storm water management challenges were all about flooding. You'll see a lot of photos from events like 1972's Hurricane Agnes of cities like Easton under water. Only the tops of the street signs are visible. Engineers and municipal planners were worried

I care deeply about the health of our community and the nature around us. There's so much to love about the Lehigh Valley.

about flooding, and a lot of time and money was spent preventing it.

Once we got a handle on major flooding, we realized that small problems can be big problems, too. We saw streams eroding their banks causing degradation of water quality. Pennsylvania is known for the miles and quality of its steams. A litmus test of stream health is fish population, and Pennsylvania streams had large trout populations we wanted to protect.

As a result, the focus of storm water management began to shift.

Today, as a civil engineer and site designer, I'm responsible for developing anything five feet outside of a building. I help to lay out the building site. I determine where the utilities will enter the site. And I design stormwater management systems because building any new structure changes the rate, volume and water quality of runoff from a site. These changes affect the health of fish—and ultimately of people. I have to strike the difficult balance of respecting a property owner's right to develop their property while still protecting the health of the local ecosystem to the best of my ability. As the effects of climate change become more apparent and we experience more frequent intense storms, stormwater management will once again have to shift to keep protecting health and property.

One of the best parts of my job is my ability to protect that health. I care deeply about the health of our community and the nature around us. There's so much to love about the Lehigh Valley. My husband, daughter, and I love to be outside in nature, walking, hiking, and biking, often in the state park five minutes from our home. We're also fortuitously located close to New York City and Philadelphia so we can easily go to the city to see a show. I love this area. I feel fortunate that my life's work is to help protect it.

The quality of our streams is important, especially for people here in the Lehigh Valley, because a lot of the Lehigh Valley relies on drinking water that comes out of the ground—from streams and wells. Water is a cycle. It's not consumptive. Water is always somewhere in the water cycle: In the simplest terms, it rains, hits the ground, runs off, gets to a stream, flows to a lake or ocean, evaporates, and then the cycle begins again. At some point in that cycle, people might use the water for drinking or washing. It makes sense the cleaner we keep the water in our streams, the better for all of our health.

The importance of safe drinking water seems so obvious, but we are all so busy, who has the time to worry about it? (Well, except storm water management engineers!) One of the best parts of my job is educating people. I love taking this technical information and distilling it and making it accessible to everyone. I often present to builders, contractors, and planning boards. These busy people need to understand how and why storm water management is important.

What's your top business tip?

Hone your speaking skills. Growing up I was very shy. When I was in college, my Dad said, "You're going to be an engineer, so you need to learn how to speak to people. Most technical people cannot easily convey information, but if you can, it will set you apart."

Upon his advice, I took a public speaking class in college, which was absolute torture for me, but it was the best thing I ever did. As I progressed through my career, my ability to speak in public has paid off in spades.

I highly recommend taking opportunities to speak in public or joining a speaking group like Toastmasters.

When and how did you find courage to take a chance?

At the end of 2021, Reuther+Bowen reached out to me. Their headquarters is in Scranton, but they wanted to bring their skills to the Lehigh Valley market. They chose me to head the new office.

I was initially unsure, but my husband said, "If you don't take this opportunity, you'll regret it. You have to go for it!"

That bolstered my confidence to take the leap. And I'm so grateful I did. It's been exciting to see how many potential clients have reached out to me and how many new jobs we've landed. My new office is so busy I hired a graduate engineer. We've doubled in size in less than six months!

We work with many different type of clients, including several local universities, hospitals and industrial and commercial clients. Partnering with universities is especially rewarding because they often have a focus on sustainability and are environmentally friendly because their students value that.

How do you put people at ease?

People tell me that I seem to have it all together. I strive to remain calm and collected because it helps my clients relax too. But my secret? I'm like a duck on a pond: I look calm on the surface, but just under the water my feet are kicking furiously!

I Build Communities and Help Them Thrive

Austin James, Digital Wizard, Brand Collabs Leader and Founding CEO of the Times Live Media Group, in Nazareth

'm a salesman by nature. As a kid, I was a model and actor. I had the opportunity to work on shoots for companies like Nabisco, Betty Crocker, and McDonald's. I even did a photoshoot with Ritz Bits crackers. At age 13, I wanted to be like the celebrities I would see on TV and in the industry that I was exposed to, seeing them jet around, on camera and having fun wherever they went, not knowing what the industry was really like until I grew older. Back then, I figured that meant being on TV—because we hadn't yet conceived of social media.

But when I was around 21, social media influencers began popping up. I remember being impressed by these new social celebrities who skillfully exerted control over their own brands, images, and careers. *That's brilliant*, I thought. Early on, people likely thought being a social media influencer was just a flash in the pan. Today it's a career.

From the beginning of social media, I saw tremendous value in Facebook groups in particular. I recognized that groups are the most interactive part of the platform. In 2018, I launched a Facebook group called the Nazareth Times. I quickly gained more than 7,000 followers.

My group grew quickly. As I promoted Nazareth, I got pitched to start a merch line and podcast show, which we did. We started promoting events, sharing news, and creating quality digital content for the community to stay up to date on all the latest and greatest news, food, and entertainment. From there it grew and grew. After that, I started a partnership with a publishing house with five direct mail publications in the region, and the brand exploded. I find people in the Lehigh Valley area—a mix of people from all different backgrounds and cultures—is what makes it so great here. We want good food, entertainment, culture, and education for our kids. But, most of all we want a great area to raise our families and develop our careers.

At the time, I was still working at a more traditional job I went to school for. I was at a crossroads. I knew I could continue working for other people, be an employee forever, or I could start my own business and chart my own course. I had to sacrifice my cushy job to start building something not so big or cushy—at least to start! I really struggled that first year, and I had to give up a lot. But I knew if I stuck with it, I could build my company. I knew I had to do it.

In 2019, one of my posts hit 400,000 people in 12 hours. After that, Facebook invited me to be part of its exclusive program called Facebook Protect, which offers tighter security regulations for high-volume groups. I was then invited to join their Facebook Community Learning Labs (FCLL), a group of around 1,500 nationwide influencers. Facebook was pushing me to become a certified Facebook Community Manager after I became the world leader on the platform in a media tool called Brand Collabs, which gives administrators of large, engaging Facebook groups the ability to target Facebook advertisers and run campaigns in our groups.

Recently, on a Zoom call, the Facebook team told me that my Nazareth Times Facebook group was the most successful group in the *world* using brand collabs. Most groups run four or five ad campaigns a month. We have hundreds!

"You're one of the most savvy and forward-thinking people we consult with on group monetization and strategic partnerships," one Facebook staffer said.

I think that I'm so successful at attracting and running these campaigns because I understand people. I offer something most traditional advertiser do not. I'm real, raw, and high energy. I understand the power of social media, human behavior, and how the mind works when using technology.

Today, I do guest speaking and education on brand collaboration, strategic partnerships, and monetization. I especially enjoy talking with kids—from middle school through college—about social media influencing. I love educating people. Our Facebook groups, publications, and podcasts all provide a service: They educate and inform. For example, one of our magazines features gluten-free recipes. People want and need those; they're hungry for it.

Another part of my company I love is the ability to help people. I want to provide value to my local community.

Social media has provided me with opportunities that have changed my life. It's opened so many doors. Over the years, my company has evolved into

I call myself a "broker of power and a trader of secrets."

Times Live Media Group. We are a multimedia brand. We specialize in print/digital media, podcast production and community/brand management. We offer a simple yet powerful way to increase a company's sales, influence, and community impact. We are media personalities with iHeart Radio and frequent guest speakers at Facebook roundtables and forums. We help our clients keep their brands alive in the eyes of the community.

Today we manage about a dozen Facebook communities (including the Nazareth Times, Lehigh Valley Food, and Fort Worth Foodies), five publications (including Lehigh Valley Food Magazine), and a dozen podcasts (including Lehigh Valley Food and Lehigh Valley Business with our production partners at Rum Runnas Entertainment). A few weeks ago, iHeart radio recruited us to do a show called Lehigh Valley Food with our partner admin.

What are the challenges of a business like yours? Working with technology has many challenges, but sometimes they pale in comparison to working with people. I call myself a "broker of power and a trader of secrets." (I got that from a movie, lol.) On social media, we're always in the public eye. Especially on social media, people can spot fakeness a mile away. Any hint of inauthenticity turns people off. To put my clients at ease and to build enduring partnerships, I'm always honest. I give people realness. No BS.

What's your greatest strength?

I think that my insight is my strongest attribute. I'm savvy, and I can always think 10 steps ahead. I'm also strong willed and have extremely thick skin and can think on my feet.

What's your hope for the future?

With the Metaverse launching, the sky's the limit with Facebook groups. I think my role is just beginning. I've been asked to speak in 2022 at the Facebook Communities Summit, which is Facebook's opportunity to bring together community builders from around the world so they can connect with one another, hear from Facebook's executives about the latest product features, and learn from each other's experiences.

On a personal note, I would love to start a foundation to help at-risk youth.

I Help People Move from Chaos to Calm and Health through Feng Shui and Building Biology

Carol Cannon, president and founder of Carol Cannon Group

I've had the same vision for decades that holds true today. I want to help people. I began practicing Feng Shui and Building Biology in the 1990s. After working 13 years in the corporate world, it was life altering to know that we could look at our houses and our offices and make changes to impact our lives.

I added Himalayan singing bowls to even better enhance the spaces I worked in and, seemingly unrelated, I use QuickBooks training to help bring a different type of calm to small business owners.

I grew up in a small village in Pennsylvania, and even before starting the Carol Cannon Group, I've always worked with homes, buildings, and land. After college, I decided to go into real estate and became a commercial real estate appraiser. I was so excited to look at land and envision what could go on it and how much it was worth.

Joining Chase Manhattan Bank took me to New York City, where I appraised proposed commercial properties for construction loans as a Vice President. It was in NYC while working at Chase that I learned about the harms of sick building syndrome. Although my building was brand new, it was completely sealed up. I found myself sick often and dealing with chronic sinusitis. Later, I ended up in Florida to manage a Chase Commercial Appraisal office in another new building in Boca Raton. The experience opened my mind to why it is so important to build and create spaces that enhance our health rather than hurt it.

By 1993, I knew it was time to take a new direction in my life. I went to school for architecture and interior design and worked for a designer briefly,

but something set me on a different path. I picked up a book on Feng Shui and interior design and read it from cover to cover in less than 24 hours. I knew instantly that Feng Shui, the Chinese art of placement, was the direction I wanted to go in.

The basic goal of practicing Feng Shui is to create an environment that allows the flow of chi, or energy, to smoothly flow through a space. Doing so helps us feel positive, healthy, and enhances our lives.

I went to California to study under the teacher of the author of the book that I read. There, I learned about the Tibetan Buddhist school of Feng Shui that had been westernized. Later, I traveled the world to learn the Classical school of Feng Shui, which is more analytical and based on direction. Today, I'm a certified Feng Shui practitioner through the New York School of Feng Shui. I also founded the Florida School of Feng Shui.

Two years later, I discovered Bau-Biologie, which is the study of how a building's environment affects the health of people in and around it. After graduating from the International Institute for Bau-Biologie and Ecology, I became a certified Building Biology Environmental Consultant.

I've had many clients who were very physically sick and didn't know why. With my training, I can go into my clients' homes and find out what's wrong. I'll notice that the bed is against the wall where the power comes into the house or next to a pool pump. I've found mold, discovered gas leaks, and pinpointed electrical fields that could be affecting my clients' health.

There's so much Feng Shui and Building Biology can do to make a space calm, peaceful, and comfortable. It begins the moment you walk into a space. Adding a water fountain to a designated space, for instance, often attracts prosperity.

One of my clients was a CFO of a company. Soon after we finished setting up his office using Feng Shui techniques, his business started bringing in more money. He told me, "I think that worked."

My typical clients:

I have clients in Pennsylvania, Florida, and all over the country. I also have clients around the world, including Singapore, Australia, and Central America.

I've noticed over the years that my clients tend to share a unique characteristic: They meditate. Typically, when people want a Feng Shui consultation—whether it's a large company or individual clients—they have some type of spiritual belief. And they want to make the best of their space for themselves, their employees, and their clients.

How Himalayan singing bowls became part of my business:

Singing bowls are healing, and their sounds penetrate to clear a space. I

There's so much Feng Shui and Building Biology can do to make a space calm, peaceful, and comfortable. It begins the moment you walk into a space. Adding a water fountain to a designated space, for instance, often attracts prosperity.

use metal Himalayan singing bowls to clear spaces that may have negative energy. Part of Feng Shui is about learning who lived in your space before you. I found that many of my clients in Pennsylvania, in particular, had homes that needed to be cleared, perhaps because of the history of the area. Although it's not a large part of my business, I also lead guided meditations with singing bowls in yoga studios, Buddhist centers, churches, and even hospitals.

And why QuickBooks?

I was an Accounting/Business major in college, and have an affinity for QuickBooks Online. It's miraculous to me that a company's finances can be organized with the click of a mouse. Some small business owners are afraid to do their own books, so I offer QuickBooks training to help them take control of their books. Helping clients to alleviate financial chaos is another way to create calm.

I'm a visionary with more plans for my business:

I stand out because I think beyond what we see right in front of us. I'm a verified double right-brained person who's capable of working with the left side of my brain. I believe that if you imagine things, you can manifest them. Decades ago, I had a vision that I was speaking to thousands of people that needed help in their lives. I have a template that I'm working on that involves expanding my business further into the digital world. So many people are filled with anxiety and feel rather hopeless. My current goal is to be able to share my knowledge in a way that is accessible to all, regardless of financial means. I want to see a world where everyone will experience peace and be able to go from Chaos to Calm!

I Help People Bring Their Innovations to Life

Katie Kupstas, CEO of Inventors Club for Women,
Wynnewood, PA

I was born and raised in the Lehigh Valley. My family has owned businesses in the Lehigh Valley for the past 60+ years. Lehigh Valley natives know the most famous of them all, the Beef House in Bethlehem. It was an innovative place and ahead of its time with the first open kitchen behind the bar. They were made famous for their roast beef and ham sandwiches. My grandparents also purchased Westport Grove later to be known as Saucon Valley Acres and owned by my parents during my childhood years. It was known for its large dance hall situated on 7 acres of beautiful landscape with fields and Saucon Creek running through it. My childhood was immersed in entrepreneurism and all the freedom and hard work that go along with it.

Growing up, I wanted to be a journalist and then in high school I wanted to be an environmental lawyer. I had done an independent study my senior year that focused on children, streams, and science. That really got me involved with helping to save the environment and things of that nature, but it was really a self-starter type project. I worked on it with a few other students at Saucon Valley High School led by environmental science teacher Lance Lenhardt. It was an entrepreneurial type project and an independent study teaching elementary school students about the health of streams. This introduced a love of teaching for me and it became my first career.

I moved to the DC Metro area in the year 2000 and it changed my life. I transferred out of Shippensburg University to George Mason University. I lived there with my now husband, Tod Kupstas. We were married in 2001. We were newly married living about a half mile from the Pentagon on September 11th. He was working at the United States Patent and Trademark Office at the time. I heard the blast from our apartment. I jumped into the car to pick him up at work to find his buildings covered in smoke. I was terrified. 9/11 was a terrible day for everyone.

Changing the lives of women to empower them to be financially independent is important to me. I want to make a difference for my family and I want to show my daughters that women can do all the things that men can do.

It made us realize how close we were to the center of the world. It was scary but also empowering. We were able to help firsthand in the coming days after 9/11. We knew we were making a difference because we were awarded certificates from the Department of Justice for helping.

We left the DC area in 2003 but treasured our time there, the experiences we had, and the friends we made. We moved back to PA to start a family. We moved to a suburb outside Philadelphia called Drexel Hill. We lived there for 9 years before spending the next few years moving a lot. We moved to the Lehigh Valley for a bit, Orlando and now finally back to the Philadelphia area. All of the moves allowed my family and I to make new friends along the way and build an amazing network not only for us as adults but for our children, too.

After teaching a few years in PA, I went onto become a sales leader for women in a female led company, starting with them in the early days of their company now known as Stella & Dot. They changed womens' lives for the better and I was excited to be part of that. I saw it transform the lives of women all over the United States and the world because the founder and CEO Jessica Herin had an idea that soon became a reality through the help of startup capital, having the right tools to create a company that has ultimately changed lives of women and families everywhere.

My time with Stella & Dot for more than a decade has been part of my inspiration that has led me to where I am today. Changing the lives of women to empower them to be financially independent is important to me. I want to make a difference for my family, and I want to show my daughters that women can do all the things that men can do with access to the same resources such as funding, attorneys and quality information that will lead them to the same success as their male counterparts.

My time serving in public relations and as an events specialist for nonprofits and tech startups has given me the opportunity to form relationships with leaders all over the world. I have worked with fashion companies such as YSL and Ralph Lauren. My diverse background brings a multitude of experience and empathy to the table that is necessary to work through the process of bringing a product to market successfully. *Knowledge is power. My joy comes from being able to share it with others.*

I believe in integrity. I wanted a company that was going to provide quality information to people that need it the most. This group of people are women. I wanted them to have access to the best information to make their products the most successful. Giving inventors the tools they need to move their business forward while saving money is one of the many reasons our members are part of the ICW community. I believe that education is the key to success. Avoiding mistakes like predatory companies, knowing how, where and when to spend your money is going to save aggravation and money in the long run.

When women entrepreneurs succeed, we all succeed. I believe in women visionaries because they account for improved economic growth which leads to more job opportunities and increased likelihood of success for other women business founders.

I am fortunate to have Tod Kupstas, Lehigh Valley native, fellow Saucon Valley Alum 1993, former patent examiner and intellectual property attorney for 20 years, as a member of my team in business and in life. He has been my spouse for 21 years and we have created a beautiful life and family together. Tod inspired me to create the company known as Inventors Club for Women. He has become an asset to our inventors in helping to secure their intellectual property while explaining to them what they need the most. As the father of both our girls he wants them to without a doubt have all the same benefits in life as our son will have. He is a former patent examiner at the United States Patent and Trademark Office. He is able to give inventors a full understanding of what type of patent or trademark they need for the most successful outcome. Tod has helped countless female friends of mine do patent searches and explain the process to them before they considered moving forward.

I am passionate about making women see the power within themselves as not only inventors but as eventual CEO's of their companies. "It is a journey and a struggle to carry the load every woman is expected to carry while also achieving professional success. My goal is to guide them to the most effective path to bring their product to market that will be the most profitable for them in the long run."

Favorite quote:

"When you learn, teach. When you get, give." Maya Angelou

I Capture and Preserve Life's Most Special Moments

Terree O'Neill Oakwood, photographer and owner of
The Moment Photography, in the Lehigh Valley

I have always been a people person. I especially enjoy talking with people and learning their stories.

My fascination with people's stories naturally evolved into a love of photographing them. I've had a camera in my hand since I was eight years old. On school field trips, the other kids had Kodak Instamatics, but I brought my professional grade camera with a long lens. It was large and cumbersome, but it took fantastic pictures.

I grew up in Philadelphia, and then I lived in Bucks County, before settling here in Lehigh County. When I was starting my family, I wanted a career that would allow me to stay home with my three kids. A photography business seemed like the perfect fit.

My company name, The Moment Photography, was inspired by a painting called The Moment. The painting is of a Native American brave and his wife nestled in each other's arms with their eyes closed, absolutely comforted by each other's presence. That painting is a treasure because it captures a moment in time and the feeling.

Much like that painting, I believe photos are treasures because they too can capture a moment and a feeling and share it with the audience. Ever since, I've photographed thousands of people in beautiful moments.

My three favorite subjects always were my two daughters, Autumn and Sequoya, and my son, Hunter. Tragically, Hunter in 2021.

Since the loss of my son, I've been interviewing and photographing other mothers who have lost children. I'm gathering their wisdom on coping with this enormous loss and carrying on to have meaningful lives. I hope to share it all in a book. The working title is Collateral Beauty because of the unexpectedly tender loving bits of beauty that have occurred around our losses

It doesn't matter if you're photographing someone on a cloudy day if they are lit up from within!

and through our connections. I focus on the good of what other people have shared with me. I hope that I can turn the collateral damage from my son's death into collateral beauty. I want to share other people's stories because if you walk into the darkness with a lit candle, the light expands. I feel that my son is with me on this project, guiding and supporting me.

Today, I continue to run The Moment Photography, especially doing corporate and family portraiture. Many of my clients are companies who need updated photos of their teams. I used to do a gamut of types of photography, literally everything, but lately I've narrowed my scope to projects that bring me the right energy.

Shooting the photos for this book series is great fun, for instance. I love meeting and photographing all of these Local Luminaries. They come to my home studio to have their photos taken. I put them at ease and get to know them, so they'll get remarkable portraits.

I also enjoy nature photography. I sometimes feel as if I am a camera. When I see beauty, I must take a picture of it. For instance, sunrises happen every day, but every day they're different. When I'm driving in the morning while the sun is coming up, I have to pull to the side of the road to document it.

How do you set people at ease to capture the best moments?

I always bring my best with my camera. Taking someone's photo is a very personal experience. It's not an ordinary job. It's very engaging, very personal. Sometimes people are nervous, worried about how their photos will come out.

Fortunately, I'm able to connect with others easily, I think because I'm such a people person. I ask a lot of questions. It's authentic because I genuinely care and want to get to know them. As I ask them questions and they answer, we always find common ground.

Another strength of mine is getting along with everyone and making them feel comfortable. This level of comfort leads to happy, relaxed expressions and faces.

I ask people to take a breath and try to relax. I say, "I promise: You don't have to worry because I'm going to take the best photos of you. Let your fears go, and we'll create something fun together!"

I ask people what they are interested in, what they're passionate about. When they answer, they light up! It doesn't matter if you're photographing someone on a cloudy day if they are lit up from within!

How do you learn and perfect your craft?

I've always believed in the importance of investing in high quality tools of the trade. For example, I buy the fastest lenses that I can afford.

Early on, I joined the Delaware Valley Guild of Photographers to interact with other photographers. I learned from exceptionally talented photographers, many who invented their own techniques.

Over time, I incorporated their techniques into my toolbox, and I also developed my own personal style. I'm captivated by romance and poetry, and I bring that into my work. I'm inspired by what other people bring to the worlds of film, songs, books, and speech. Whatever stirs my soul, I bring that emotion into my photography.

What are your future goals?

I want to write books of value that are helpful for others and combine my photography with my writing.

I also have a passion for photographing moments of ordinary life. I've been collecting these slices of life, such as a shot of a very old woman in Buenos Aires hanging her wet clothing on a second story laundry line. Another photo is of two men in their sixties chilling on their front porch. A third is an image of a dozen old men sitting on benches outside a donut shop on the boardwalk, wearing T-shirts and ballcaps, laughing and telling stories. I'm fascinated by ordinary life. Every day, people are doing the best that they can to live their lives. I think that's brilliant.

ABOUT THE
Local Luminaries

We are pleased to present the Local Luminaries' and curators' business and contact information here, in alphabetical order.

Valerie Bittner

Actor, Model, Voice Artist

www.valeriebittner.com

610-248-0066

valeriebittner@aim.com

Services offered: On-camera talent/ spokesperson, commercial print model, and voice over artist

Discount for readers: 10% off

Jennifer Bright

Founder/CEO, Bright Communications

www.BrightCommunications.net

610-216-0913

Jennifer@BrightCommunications.net

Services offered: Book publishing, brochure and promotion piece creation, website content developing, and publishing and author coaching

Discount: 10% discount on publishing packages

Carol Cannon

President and Founder of Carol Cannon Group

www.carolcannongroup.com

484-951-0926

Carol@CarolCannonGroup.com

LinkedIn: linkedin.com/in/
carolcannongroup

Facebook: @CarolCannonGroup

Services offered: Feng Shui consulting for existing or proposed commercial and residential properties in person or via Zoom.

Michael Carnathan, MD

Owner/Physician, Arrow Primary Care

https://arrowprimarycare.com

484-626-0121

drmike@arrowprimarycare.com

2223 Linden Street, Suite 2 Bethlehem, PA 18017

Services offered: Family medicine services in a direct primary care model

Amanda Morris D'Agostino, PhD

Artist

www.amandadagostinoart.com

610-628-1279

amandadagostinoart@gmail.com

Instagram: @amandadagostinoart

Facebook: facebook.com/AmandaDPhotoArt

Services offered: Original oil paintings, prints, notecards, and accepts commissions

Discount for readers: 25% off first commissioned art

Carmen S. Dancsecs

Client Relationship Manager at First United Closing

www.FirstUnitedClosing.com

610-433-0432

carmen@firstunitedclosing.com

3500 Winchester Rd. Suite 202 Allentown, PA 18104

Services offered: Title and settlement services

Nelson A. Diaz

President, Mi Casa Properties

610-442-6765

nadiaz4413@outlook.com

1129 W Linden Street, 1st Floor, Allentown, PA 18102

Services offered: Real estate rentals and sales

Mi Casa Es Su Casa

1129 W Linden Street, 1st fl
Allentown, Pa 18102
610-442-6765

Laura M. Eberly, PE, LEED AP

Director of Civil Engineering – Lehigh Valley

www.reutherbowen.com

484-403-1560

leberly@reutherbowen.com

2980 Linden Street, Unit C2, Bethlehem, PA 18017

Services offered: Civil engineering and land planning, structural engineering for buildings, structural detailing of steel shop drawings, building information modeling (BIM) / integrated project delivery (IPD), forensic engineering, and construction engineering

Engineering, Design, Construction Services

Neville Gardner

Owner of Donegal Square and McCarthy's Red Stag Pub & Whiskey Bar

www.donegalsquare.com and www.redstagpub.com

610-866-3244 (Donegal Square) and 610-861-7631 (McCarthy's Red Stag Pub)

info@doengalsquare.com and info@redstagpub.com

Instagram: @donegalsquare and @redstagpub

Facebook: @DonegalSq and @McCarthysBethlehem

534 Main Street, Bethlehem, PA 18018

Services offered: Donegal Square offers the best from Ireland and the British Isles with authentic, handcrafted goods from the Celtic lands, including Nicholas Mosse Irish Pottery, Shanore handcrafted Irish jewelry, Keith Jack's unique jewelry designs, and our full line of handknit Irish sweaters for both men and women.

At McCarthy's Red Stag Pub and Whiskey Bar, you'll experience a taste of Ireland and the British Isles, with authentic Irish and British Isles food made from scratch, a full bar, an extensive whiskey menu, and a family-friendly atmosphere.

Patty Gatter

Founder and CEO, The Breastfeeding Shop

www.thebreastfeedingshop.com

908-581-2153

patty@thebreastfeedingshop.com

Services offered: Breast pumps, accessories, and telehealth

Julio A. Guridy

Director of the Contract Compliance Programs at the Delaware River
Joint Toll Bridge Commission

www.DRJTBC.org

215-528-1108

JGuridy@DRJTBC.org

Services offered: Bridges crossings over the Delaware River between
PA and NJ

Rita Guthrie

Owner/idea lady, Open Door Public Relations

www.opendoorlv.com

610-703-5878

idealady@opendoorlv.com

Services offered: Consulting in strategic marketing and public
relations for small business, public speaking, brand consistency,
establishing co-marketing partnerships, business event concepts

Amanda Hecker

Owner, Diversity Training and Education

www.AmandaPorter.net

215-237-4191

amandaglynn1@gmail.com

Services offered: Transgender specific training, education, and consulting services in Diversity, Equity, and Inclusion

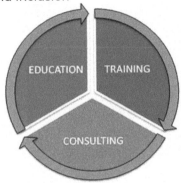

Louis Wyker Holzman

B2B Marketing Sales and Strategy, Non-Profit Activist, and Real Estate Investor

https://altitudemarketing.com and www.allentownyoungprofessionals.org

610-674-2870

louis@queencityrealty.net

Services offered: Sales consulting, marketing strategy, real estate acquisition and management, and administrative and operational consulting

Lyn Hufton, AHWD, ABR, SRS, CMRS

Realtor, Berkshire Hathaway Home Services, Fox and Reach Realtors

Lynhufton.foxroach.com

610-762-0670

Lyn.hufton@foxroach.com

Services offered: Work with residential home buyers and sellers in Lehigh, Northampton, Berks, and Bucks Counties

Austin James

CCM, Meta Chief Community Officer

www.timeslivemediagroup.com

timeslivemedia@gmail.com

25 S Main Street, Nazareth, PA 18064

Services offered: Print/digital marketing, podcast production, community management, drone and video production, reel promotions, influence marketing, and radio promotions for iHeartMedia.

Julie Knight, CFP®, AIF®, CLTC®, CDFA®

First Vice President/Wealth Management, Financial Advisor

www.klcwealthadvisory.com

610-674-6981

julieknight@janney.com

1390 Ridgeview Drive, Suite 101, Allentown, PA 18104

Services offered: Comprehensive wealth management services: financial planning, estate planning, retirement planning, investing, education planning, asset protection, long-term care and life insurance

For more information about Janney, please see Janney's Relationship Summary (Form CRS) on www.janney.com/discloure/crs which details all material facts about the scope and terms of our relationship with you and any potential conflicts of interest.

Katie Kupstas

CEO, Inventors Club for Women

inventorsclubforwomen.com

katie@inventorsclubforwomen.com

Instagram: @inventorsclubworldwide

@katies.clicks

Facebook: @KatieKupstas
LinkedIn: @KatieKupstas

Services offered: Guiding members from inventor to founder to CEO through the process of bringing a product to market and seeing the value of intellectual property as an asset to their company.

Michelle Landis

President/Owner, Pinnacle 7

www.pinnacle7.com

610-438-4666

michellelandis@pinnacle7.com

Services offered: Leadership and business coaching and consulting

Discount for readers: 10%

Joanne Leasure

Owner, Day One Accounting and Financial Services, LLC

http://dayoneaccounting.com

800-587-5554

joanne@dayoneaccounting.com

Instagram: @dayoneaccounting

Linkedin: https://www.linkedin.com/in/joannejohnsonleasure/

2785 Route 115, Suite 101, Effort, PA 18330

Services offered: We fix broken bookkeeping and accounting systems and coach business owners to multiply their revenue.

David C. Myers

Vice President, Human Resources, Jetson Specialty Marketing Services, Inc. (JSM) Direct Mail Services

484-772-4011

dave.myers@jsmsi.com

CEO/CHRO, Human Asset Strategies

Easton, PA

610-751-8150

davchmyers@gmail.com

LinkedIn: @davidcmyers1

Services offered: Human resources/organizational development consulting

Terree O'Neill Oakwood

Photographer, Writer, and Owner, The Moment Photography

www.TheMomentPhoto.com

215-264-6136

terreeo.beautifulmoments@gmail.com

Services offered: Portrait, event, and branding photography

Pete Reinke

Assistant Vice President, Business Development Officer

www.univest.net

610-442-9398

reinkep@univest.net

Services offered: Banking, insurance, investments, integrated client strategies, tailored financial solutions

Byron Roth

Owner, TAB Lehigh Valley and B Roth Consulting

www.TABLehighValley.com

908-391-4776

broth@tablehighvalley.com

Services offered: Business coaching, exit planning, and consulting services

Robert Sayre

Founder, SRS Real Estate Investments, LLC

www.linkedin.com/in/rob-sayre-3559772

Robert.sayre1@gmail.com

Facebook: @Robert.Sayre1

Twitter: Rsayre5615

Services offered: We can buy your property with cash. We solve problems that seem unsolvable. We can show you how to use real estate to create legacy wealth.

Liz P. Summers

Founder and President, Advancing Leadership Consulting, Inc.

www.AdvancingLeadershipConsulting.com

336-312-7325

LSummers@AdvancingLeadershipConsulting.com

LinkedIn: @LizSummers

Services offered: Transformative leadership coaching and facilitation for individuals and organizations.

ADVANCING LEADERSHIP

George Wacker

Owner, Lehigh Valley with Love Media

https://linktr.ee/lvwithlove

484-554-2234

info@lehighvalleywithlovemedia.com

Services offered: Digital media, video, podcasting, digital events, social media, consultation, marketing, public relations

Terry Wallace

CEO, Alynus Inc and Venture X Lehigh Valley

www.venturex.com

484-403-0077

terry.wallace@venturex.com

306 S. New Street, Bethlehem, PA 18015

List of Services offered: Office space, amenities, and business services

Discount for readers: Free day pass

Jane Wells-Schooley

CEO, internationally certified executive coach, and educator, Northstar Team Development

www.NorthstarTeamDevelopment.com

610-390-9000

janews@northstarteamdevelopment.com

Instagram: @janewellsschooley

Facebook: @NorthstarTeamDevelopment

Twitter: @NorthstarTeams and @Northstar_Women

Services offered: Executive and leadership coaching, leadership development classes and mentoring for age group 18 to 29 including financial education, and group facilitation using experiential education

Maria Wirth

Co-Founder and Managing Director, Business Owners Trade Alliance

www.botatrade.com

484-225-6063

mwirth@botatrade.com

Services offered: The benefits of buying and selling with trade dollars instead of cash. Members enjoy barter purchasing power with participating local businesses and a marketplace with 75,000 members for worldwide vacations and other products and services.

Discount for readers: $95 off membership for qualifying businesses

Jayme Zick

Co-Owner/Operations Manager, The Settlement Company

www.thesetco.com

484-892-6200

info@thesetco.com

2150 W Washington St, Allentown, PA 18104

Services offered: Title insurance and settlement services for properties located in PA and NJ.

ABOUT THE
Photographer

Terree O'Neill Oakwood is a professional photographer and entrepreneur. Twenty-eight years ago, she began The Moment Photography, creating studio and location lifestyle and branding portraits. Terree also enjoys dabbling in writing and has chronicled on Facebook the many life changes she has experienced in recent years. In so doing, she's discovered her enjoyment of inspiring others through the stories of simple life happenings. Next on her list, she hopes to combine her photography and love of writing into a book that would help others notice the wonder all around us and grow from an open-hearted approach to living.

ABOUT THE
Curators

Jennifer Bright

 Jennifer is founding CEO of Bright Communications LLC and Momosa Publishing LLC, publisher of the popular Mommy MD Guides books and dozens of other books by expert authors and visionary brands.

Jennifer is a publisher, editor, and writer with more than 25 years of publishing experience. She has contributed to more than 150 books and published more than 100 magazine and newspaper articles.

She proudly served as a lieutenant in the U.S. Army for four years, stationed at Fort Lewis, Washington. Jennifer then worked for seven years on staff at Rodale before launching her own editorial business, Bright Communications LLC.

Jennifer's passion is helping parents raise healthier, happier families. She lives in Hellertown, Pennsylvania, with her fiancé. Together, they have five pairs of chickens, four sons, three cats, two dogs, and one amazing life. She can be reached at jennifer@brightcommunications.net.

Rita Guthrie

Rita Guthrie, founder of Open Door Public Relations, has been involved in marketing, public relations, and creative business events since the early 90s. Back in the day, her colleagues nicknamed her the Idea Lady for being the go-to person for brainstorming clever PR and marketing ideas.

Open Door PR was established in 2005 with a focus on small business and start-ups. As a business-to-business consultant, Rita has helped thousands of clients increase their visibility and bottom line by seeing through the clutter and giving them what they really need.

She has a flair for making valuable connections for her clients by developing co-marketing partnerships with other businesses that deal with the same demographic. The Idea Lady helps the business owner explore a wide variety of tools to reach out, stay in touch, and arouse the curiosity of prospective clients. Her people learn to create a marketing calendar that reaches across all channels, getting the word out on their products or services by educating, entertaining, and engaging.

In addition to one-to-one consulting, Rita runs informal workshops called Coffee Talk throughout the year. These events are open to all. Each one has a specific public relations or marketing theme. Essentially, they are discussion-based networking events.

Rita Guthrie has a genuine love of connecting people and seeing small businesses grow and flourish.

A native of Brooklyn, she also lived Upstate New York and at the Jersey Shore before coming to the Lehigh Valley in 1987. Rita and her husband have three children and five grandchildren. She is a volunteer with TEDx Lehigh River, an active regular at 1 Million Cups, and serves on the Chancellor's Advisory Council for LaunchBox Ladies at Penn State LV. She practices yoga and catches up on NPR podcasts during her daily walks. Rita can be reached at idealady@opendoorlv.com.

Robert Sayre

Rob, a native of Boulder, Colorado moved to the East Coast in 1982 to work at a small book publishing company and to the Lehigh Valley in 1988 to work at Rodale, Inc. as the business manager of its book division, with many great leaders and coworkers. He is now semi-retired, an active investor in real estate, and a volunteer as a master gardener with the Penn State Extension Service, and he has studied and practiced tai chi for 11 years. He and his wife, Sally, a retired public-school teacher, have three children and five of the best grandchildren ever. They are as busy as ever, but they love controlling their own schedule and traveling in their Lance RV Camper.

Also in the Local Luminaries Series